Richness and Rarity
The Natural History of Lucas County

By Elliot Tramer

Photos by Art Weber

The University of Toledo Press

2020

The University of Toledo Press
www.utoledopress.com

Copyright 2020
By The University of Toledo Press

Richness & Rarity
The Natural History of Lucas County

Made possible with the support of

Edited by Yarko Kuk

Project assistance from Erin Czerniak, Madison Rane Vasko, and Stephanie Delo

Book design by Yarko Kuk

Cover photo: A large white oak at Blue Creek Metropark. Photo by Art Weber.

ISBN 978-1-7332664-6-8

DEDICATION

In memory of Lou Campbell and Harold Mayfield. Their knowledge of our natural history was unparalleled. Their dedication to sharing that knowledge helped make this book possible.

TABLE OF CONTENTS

ACKNOWLEDGEMENTS

First and foremost, I am especially grateful to my publisher, Yarko Kuk, Managing Editor of The University of Toledo Press, for his enthusiastic support of this project, the beautiful layout, and for significant improvements in the graphics and style.

This book was the "brain child" of Steve Madewell, former Executive Director of Metroparks Toledo. I am truly thankful to Steve for giving me an opportunity to take the leadership role in creating this book, and for giving me continuing encouragement as the project developed. That encouragement has been sustained by current Metroparks Director Dave Zenk and the Metroparks Director of Public Relations Scott Carpenter.

This project would not have been possible without the essays of nineteen guest authors, who agreed to provide essays on areas of their special expertise. Obtaining contributions from nineteen contributors can be an exercise in herding cats, but without exception, all were ready and willing to donate their time and talents to this project, without the imposition of deadlines. In alphabetical order, they are:

Kent Bekker, Tom Bridgeman, Mark Camp, Todd Crail, Jan Dixon, Eric Durbin, Ross Ellet, Tim Fisher, Kim High, Matt Horvat, Bob Jacksy, Jr., Larry Nelson, Rick Nirschl, Matthew Snyder, Carol Stepien, Amy Stone, Janet Traub, Jim Toppin, and Tim Walters.

The book has been enormously enhanced by many photographs, the vast majority provided by the superb talents of Art Weber. I am also grateful to other photo contributors, some of them local photographers. They are acknowledged individually in the photo credits in the book.

Helpful comments on portions of the text were provided by Michelle Grigore and Kim High. I am especially indebted to Erin Moan for a review of the entire manuscript.

Finally, I acknowledge the patience and unvarying support of my wife Christine Manzey, who makes all things possible for me.

Elliot Tramer

FOREWORD

Why have a book on the natural history of a single county? At first glance, one would not expect Lucas County to be remarkable for its natural resources. The terrain is largely flat, and much of the land surface is either given over to intensive agriculture or is urbanized. Toledo, Ohio's fourth-largest city, is the county seat. And yet, Lucas County is remarkably diverse. It contains more rare and threatened plant and animal species than any other county in Ohio. Its Lake Erie shoreline features extensive marshes teeming with migratory waterfowl and provides a globally significant staging area for spring-migrating songbirds. In western Lucas County, the Oak Openings contains remnants of globally rare communities such as oak savannas, sand barrens, and wet prairies. These sites harbor the majority of the county's rare plant and insect species. Finally, the Maumee River—the largest river entering the Great Lakes—passes through Lucas County and is famous for a spring walleye run that attracts fishermen from hundreds of miles away.

This book is an attempt to review, in condensed form, the natural features that make Lucas County special. Its goal is to enhance our citizens' knowledge and appreciation of those resources, so that they may be preserved for the enjoyment of generations to come. A portion of the book is also devoted to the historical events that shaped the present-day landscape, and a review of conservation challenges.

This additional material is vitally important, since the future of our natural resources is by no means guaranteed. Although the population of Lucas County has actually declined somewhat over the past 50 years, the percentage of land area converted from agriculture and open space to urban and suburban development has nearly doubled during the same time period. Other factors, such as climate change, invasive species, and water quality issues, provide additional challenges.

Fortunately, Lucas County's natural resources have a bright future. Local institutions and agencies and the general public are deeply committed to their preservation. Near the Lake Erie shore, the U.S. Fish & Wildlife Service, Ohio Department of Natural Resources (DNR) Division of Wildlife, and Metroparks Toledo manage substantial wetland and forest acreages for the benefit of wildlife and the public. West of the Maumee River, the Metroparks, The Nature Conservancy, and the Ohio DNR Divisions of Forestry and Natural Areas and Preserves have significant land holdings and provide similar benefits. The world-class Toledo Zoo & Aquarium enhances public appreciation of wildlife through its many educational programs and operates a highly successful captive breeding program with the goal of returning endangered species to the wild. There are a number of active nature-oriented organizations in the county that provide opportunities for citizens to learn more about our natural resources and become actively involved in their preservation. Finally, environmental programs at the University of Toledo and nearby Bowling Green State University offer coursework, internships, and research opportunities for the future generation of environmental professionals.

Nineteen local experts, knowledgeable about a variety of aspects of our natural environment, have contributed to this book. Their names appear in the headings of sections they have written. I have also written large portions of the book myself. Most of those sections reflect my own expertise in areas of animal and plant ecology; others are attempts to provide a general overview and transitions to help the book "hang together."

A natural history book is a snapshot of conditions as they exist at the time of writing. The environment of Lucas County has changed enormously since the first European settlers arrived 200 years ago. Change is inevitable, so it is safe to say that Lucas County will be a different place 200 years from now. But this book will continue to have value, initially as a guide to the natural features that exist today, and later as a basis for comparison as our landscape changes.

A word of explanation: Supplying scientific names for all organisms mentioned herein would vastly increase the length and make for cumbersome reading and is hopefully unnecessary for well-known species. However, they have been included in some cases, e.g., for the less familiar plant species, especially since it is not unusual for multiple common names to be applied to several (often unrelated) species.

This book is an outlet for the perspective I have gained after living in Lucas County for 50 years as an ecologist, writer and educator. I hope you enjoy reading it, and the wonderful photos Art Weber and others have provided.

Elliot Tramer

CHAPTER ONE

General Features of Lucas County

Lucas County is located in northwestern Ohio, at the southwest corner of Lake Erie. The roughly triangular western portion of the county is bounded on the south by the Maumee River and on the north by Michigan. Fulton County lies to the west. The smaller eastern portion, a panhandle-shaped projection east of the Maumee River, is bounded on the north by Lake Erie, and abuts Wood and Ottawa Counties to the south and east. With a land area of 342 square miles (218,880 acres), Lucas is the fourth-smallest of Ohio's 88 counties. The county is named after Robert Lucas, who was Governor of Ohio in 1835 when the county was first organized. Toledo, the fourth-largest city in Ohio, is the county seat.

In 2018 the U.S. Census Bureau estimated the population of Lucas County to be 429,899, with 95 percent of the population living in urban or subur-

Sunrise at Howard Marsh Metropark on the autumnal equinox in September 2018. (Photo by Art Weber)

ban settings. The population of the county has been declining gradually since it peaked in 1970. The 2000 census listed the population of Lucas County as 455,054. Between 2000 and 2018 the county lost just over 25,000 people, a decline of 5.5 percent.

Much of Lucas County is occupied by the Lake Plain, a landscape of low topographic relief extending southward from the Lake Erie shore. In western Lucas County, a strip of low sand ridges called the Oak Openings region extends from southwest to northeast, providing more relief. Elevations range from about 570 feet above sea level at the lakeshore to over 730 feet in the western portion of the county.

Aquatic Habitats

Lake Erie and the Maumee River are the county's most important aquatic features. The Maumee is the largest river entering the Great Lakes, draining a watershed that extends westward to Fort Wayne, Indiana and northward into Lenawee County, Michigan. The lower fourteen miles of the river, from the city of Maumee to its mouth, is essentially an estuary, with so little drop in elevation that the river may be blown upstream by strong northeast winds. Shallow rapids, where the river flows over limestone bedrock, occur at intervals upstream from the city of Maumee.

At Toledo the river empties into Maumee Bay, a shallow arm of Lake Erie partially enclosed by the Woodtick Peninsula on the north and Little Cedar Point on the east. Eastward from Little Cedar Point,

Lucas County extends for another ten miles along the shore of the western basin of Lake Erie. West of the river, major tributaries include Swan Creek and the Ottawa River/Tenmile Creek complex. Both traverse the entire width of the county. Swan Creek empties into the Maumee in downtown Toledo; the Ottawa River enters Maumee Bay north of the mouth of the Maumee River, near the Michigan line. Smaller tributaries, often little more than ditches, enter the lake east of the river. These include Crane, Duck, and Otter creeks.

Lake Erie is the shallowest of the Great Lakes, and this applies especially to the waters off Lucas County. Maumee Bay is so shallow it has to be dredged almost continuously during the warmer months to maintain the 28-foot-deep shipping channel into the port of Toledo. During prolonged southwest winds, surface waters of the lake are blown eastward, reducing depths in much of the Bay to just a few feet. The substrate is mostly soft sediments washed out of the Maumee River watershed, although firmer surfaces may be covered by colonies of Zebra and Quagga Mussels, introduced from Eurasia.

The lake off Lucas County is rich in aquatic life, with dense "algae" blooms peaking in late summer (the bloom organisms are actually cyanobacteria, not algae, although the name "blue-green algae" is often applied to them). Fish are abundant, with Walleye and Yellow Perch the most important sport species. Thousands of ducks cover the bay and adjacent lakeshore marshes during the peak of waterfowl migration in early spring and late fall.

Several important wetlands abut the Lake Erie

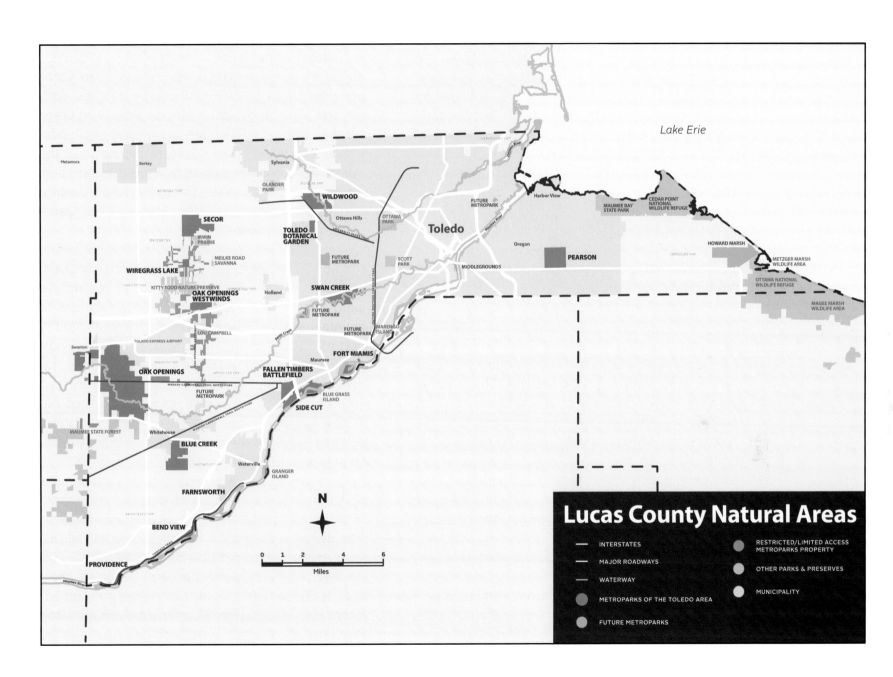

Lake Erie

Metamora · Berkey · Sylvania

OLANDER PARK

WILDWOOD

SECOR

IRWIN PRAIRIE

TOLEDO BOTANICAL GARDEN

Ottawa Hills · Ottawa Park

Toledo

FUTURE METROPARK

Harbor View

FUTURE METROPARK

MAUMEE BAY STATE PARK

CEDAR POINT NATIONAL WILDLIFE REFUGE

HOWARD MARSH

MEILKE ROAD SAVANNA

Oregon

PEARSON

METZGER MARSH WILDLIFE AREA

WIREGRASS LAKE

KITTY TODD NATURE PRESERVE

Scott Park

SCOTT PARK

MIDDLEGROUNDS

OTTAWA NATIONAL WILDLIFE REFUGE

OAK OPENINGS WESTWINDS

Holland

SWAN CREEK

FUTURE METROPARK

MAGEE MARSH WILDLIFE AREA

LOU CAMPBELL

FUTURE METROPARK

MARENGO ISLAND

Swanton

TOLEDO EXPRESS AIRPORT

Maumee

FORT MIAMIS

OAK OPENINGS

WABASH-CANNONBALL TRAIL NORTH FORK

FALLEN TIMBERS BATTLEFIELD

BLUE GRASS ISLAND

FUTURE METROPARK

WABASH-CANNONBALL TRAIL SOUTH FORK

SIDE CUT

MAUMEE STATE FOREST

Whitehouse

BLUE CREEK

Waterville

GRANGER ISLAND

FARNSWORTH

N

BEND VIEW

PROVIDENCE

Maumee River

0 1 2 4 6
Miles

Lucas County Natural Areas

— INTERSTATES

— MAJOR ROADWAYS

— WATERWAY

● METROPARKS OF THE TOLEDO AREA

● FUTURE METROPARKS

● RESTRICTED/LIMITED ACCESS METROPARKS PROPERTY

● OTHER PARKS & PRESERVES

● MUNICIPALITY

3

shore within Lucas County. Most of these were originally established by private hunting clubs, but are now managed by state or federal wildlife agencies. These include the Cedar Point National Wildlife Refuge, Metzger Marsh, Navarre Marsh, Mallard Club Marsh, swamp forests in the eastern portion of Maumee Bay State Park, and the northern portions of Magee Marsh and Ottawa National Wildlife Refuge.

Terrestrial Habitats

Visitors to Lucas County often comment on how flat the land appears, and how much of the land is treeless expanses devoted to agriculture. Actually, according to 2013 data, only about 35 percent of the land surface is farmland – mostly planted in corn, soybeans and winter wheat. About five percent is in parklands and forest, with suburban and urban housing, commercial, and institutional uses occupying the remaining 60 percent. In addition, the proportion of agricultural land is declining rapidly as farms are converted to residential subdivisions and commercial properties. While the population of Lucas County has been steadily declining, the amount of land converted from rural to suburban and urban uses has nearly doubled since 1970.

Despite the spread of development into rural areas, Lucas County retains some very special natural habitats. Most are protected within reserves, and there is a strong constituency of people actively engaged in conserving these places, as well as expanding them when private landholdings with valuable natural features become available for purchase. Special natural landscapes include several rare habitats within the oak openings region, wooded corridors along the Maumee River and other major streams, and the aforementioned wetlands along Lake Erie. But we need not rely solely on parks and other protected lands to provide a diverse, healthy natural environment. Many residential neighborhoods in the area provide abundant trees, shrubs, and flower gardens and are important habitats for birds, pollinating insects, and other wildlife.

Climate of Lucas County
By Ross Ellet

Climate may be defined as an average of the prevailing weather conditions that takes place year after year. Northwest Ohio's temperate-zone latitude allows the area to enjoy four full and distinct seasons. Large bodies of water can moderate a region's climate. But since our area is hundreds of miles away from the Gulf of Mexico, Atlantic, and Pacific Oceans, our temperatures have large seasonal variation. The lack of a mountain range to our south allows ample moisture and humidity to reach the area, since most of our precipitation arrives as moisture evaporated from the Gulf of Mexico. That in turn allows the county to receive frequent precipitation. Toledo's weather records, which go back to the late 1870s, show a wide range of extremes. Floods, droughts, tornadoes, hail, blizzards, ice jams, extreme heat, and arctic cold are just some of the weather threats that can occur in Lucas County.

Our climate classification is humid continental. A humid continental climate has large seasonal temperature differences with hot summers and cold winters. Showers and storms make up most of the summer-time precipitation. The severe weather season can start as early as March and at times lasts through the summer season. The peak severe weather season in the county is from the middle of May through the middle of July. May, June, and July are also the wettest months of the year. The hot and humid summer weather leads to the most active and vivid lightning displays of the year. Between June 1 and August 31 each year, lightning is observed on an average of twenty individual days at the Toledo Express Airport. The other nine months of the year average only eighteen thunderstorm days.

Lightning over the interurban bridge near Farnsworth Metropark. (Photo by Art Weber)

The summer season can also bring extreme heat at times. Each year the county averages about fifteen 90-degree days. Since 1871 there has only been one year on record (1907) when the summer temperature did not reach 90 degrees. The dust bowl years in the middle 1930s brought dry and hot summers, especially in 1934 and 1936. The hottest day in Toledo was July 14, 1936 when the temperature hit 105 degrees. The mid-1950s brought several seasons of extreme heat, but perhaps the most memorable summer in modern times was the drought of 1988. That summer broke the record for 90-degree days. In 1988 44 days topped 90 degrees, and five of those days reached or surpassed 100 degrees. Another heat wave in 1995 killed more than 500 people in Chicago and also brought oppressive conditions to northern Ohio. The 59-year anniversary of Toledo's hottest day brought the second hottest day on record with a temperature of 104 degrees on July 14, 1995. The heat index (a measure combining temperature and relative humidity) topped out between 120 and 130 degrees.

Late summer is typically the sunniest time of the year in northwest Ohio. From late July through early October, the rain amounts and frequency slowly drop, and the atmosphere is typically more stable. October brings colorful fall foliage and the first frosty nights of the season. The earliest freeze ever recorded in the fall season was on September 14, 1975; the latest first freeze on record was on November 15. October 18 is the average first freeze date. The first measurable snow typically falls a little over a month later, at the end of November.

The winter season is the most variable and wild time of the year. Early winter is also the cloudiest. Frequent areas of low pressure bring widespread clouds, and the Great Lakes reinforce the clouds from November into January. All summer long the sun has been warming the Great Lakes. Since it takes a lot longer for a large body of water to change temperature compared to the surrounding land, the Great Lakes become a source of instability and moisture when arctic air moves over them. The warm and moist air rises quickly in arctic air, creating convection. Since the wind typically moves out of the north, northwest, or west when cold air is moving across the area, a heavy lake-effect snow may occur near eastern Lake Erie, most commonly from Cleveland, Ohio to Buffalo, New York.

Lucas County rarely experiences heavy lake effect snows. Even though we live along the Lake Erie lakeshore, our weather is often generated from Lake Michigan during the early winter. We live too far away to see heavy lake-effect snowfall on a regular basis, although snow flurries and clouds are very common, most often occurring when low atmospheric pressure cells pass through the region.

Winter can be mild or wild in Lucas County. While many dream of a white Christmas, the odds of having heavy rain and thunderstorms on Christmas Eve or Christmas Day are about the same as getting a snowstorm. The county gets a little of everything.

Facing page: Frost on the Girdham Road dunes at Oak Openings Preserve Metropark. (Photo by Art Weber)

The Blizzard of 1978 was a powerful superbomb that parparalyzed the region for days. (Photos Courtesy *The Blade*)

The season as a whole brings about 35 to 40 inches of snow each year. Only 12.2 inches of snow fell in the winter of 1918-19 which is the least amount ever recorded. On the other hand, 86.3 inches of snow fell during the record-setting winter of 2013-14. Of course, when it comes to winter memories, nothing stands out more than a big snowstorm or blizzard. A blizzard has more to do with wind and blowing snow than the amount of snow that falls. Snow must be falling or blowing, with winds at or over 35 mph, and visibility at or under quarter of a mile for at least three hours to be classified as a blizzard.

There have been many storms with near blizzard conditions in Lucas County over the past several decades, but nothing in modern times compares with the Blizzard of 1978. That storm was a powerful superbomb (a weather term for a rapidly intensifying storm rarely seen in the Midwest). On January 26, 1978 life literally came to a standstill across the county, state, and region. Two storm systems collided over the Ohio River Valley. One storm brought warm, moist air from the Gulf of Mexico, while the second storm brought an incredible amount of cold air and wind from Canada. The combined storm brought even more wind. It is widely believed that winds gusted to 60 mph across Lucas County. There was a wind measurement over Lake Erie close to Cleveland that was well over 100 mph. The storm brought snow which changed to freezing rain, then rain and back again to snow. The official records at Toledo Express airport show 13.3 inches of snow that fell from January 25 to January 27. By January 28, 1978, the snow depth was 17 inches, as there

A young black oak tree is covered with ice after a storm. Girdham Dunes at Oak Openings Preserve Metropark. (Photo by Art Weber)

was already a heavy snowpack on the ground before the storm arrived. It is hard to determine how much snow actually fell, because the wind whipped waves of snow drifts across the land that were impossible to measure accurately.

While the Blizzard of 1978 is one of the most legendary storms to hit Lucas County in modern times, it might not have been the only storm of its kind to sweep across the region. On January 12, 1918 a blizzard packing sustained winds – for fifteen hours straight – with wind gusts between 58 and 63 mph,

hit Lucas County. Toledo only measured 8 inches of snow, but the *Toledo Blade* reported most of the area picked up 10 to 15 inches of new snow. Reports of the day went on to say drifts were 10 to 15 feet deep and covered houses, vehicles, and trains. There were also records of blizzards sweeping through the county in 1864, 1894, 1912, 1935, 1950, 1974, and 1977.

Ice storms occur every few years as well. They can do significant damage to trees and cause extensive power outages. Fog and freezing fog are also

Toledo 30 yr. Weather Averages, 1980-2010

MONTH	HIGH TEMP	LOW TEMP	PRECIP INCHES	SNOWFALL
JAN	32.7	18.7	2.05	11.6
FEB	36.2	20.9	2.07	9.4
MAR	47	28.7	2.48	5.7
APR	60.1	38.9	3.19	1.3
MAY	71.1	46.8	3.58	0.1
JUN	80.8	58.6	3.57	
JUL	84.6	62.5	3.23	
AUG	82.3	61	3.15	
SEP	75.5	52.8	2.78	
OCT	62.9	41.8	2.6	0.2
NOV	49.8	33.3	2.86	1.9
DEC	36.4	23.2	2.68	7.4

common at times during the winter season. Extreme cold can also cause major problems in the heart of winter. The average season brings six days at or below 0 degrees. During the 1962-63 winter season the mercury dropped below 0 degrees on 29 different days; however, there are many years where the temperature stays above zero.

The spring warm up gets tricky in Lucas County. Lake Erie normally freezes over during the winter, and that ice and cold water act as a freezer anytime the wind is out of the east or northeast. Warm fronts can stall out across Lucas County providing temperatures in the 70s and 80s for the southwest corner of the county, while temperatures might be in the 40s and 50s along the lakeshore. The average last freeze date is April 27, but in most years the last frost normally happens in early May. While the spring is typically a calmer time of the year with more sunshine, occasionally the skies turn violent. The severe weather season doesn't peak until late spring into early summer. However, the county's most violent tornado outbreak on record occurred on Palm Sunday 1965. On April 11, 1965 around 9:30 p.m. a large F4 tornado tore through north Toledo and Point Place.

The Toledo Express Airport climate records show an average yearly temperature of 50 degrees. The county averages about 32.5 inches of rain each year. About 136 days each year produce some amount of precipitation, with 38 of those days considered "thunderstorm days," which means that thunder can be heard at some point during the day. The average wind speed through the year is eleven mph.

Finally, 52 percent of the daylight hours each year are sunny. See the accompanying table for Toledo weather averages, from 1980 to 2010.

Climate Trends

Climate is constantly changing. Natural cycles of solar radiation, volcanic activity, and human activities all affect our climate. Some natural processes, like volcanoes, can cool temperatures on a global scale by releasing sulfuric acid and particulate ash, which screen out solar radiation. Human activities, especially burning fossil fuels and cutting down forests, can warm the atmosphere by adding carbon dioxide and other greenhouse gases to the atmosphere. On the other hand, human activities that release sulfuric acid can have the opposite effect. Anything from farming to adding concrete, asphalt, tall buildings, or smoke stacks to the landscape can alter wind, temperature, and rainfall patterns across an area as large as Lucas County.

Toledo weather has had many ups and downs in the past 140 years. To determine whether the climate is changing, it is useful to group weather data into decade-long averages to smooth out some of the chaotic changes in weather that occur from day to day and year to year. Cold decades existed from 1885 to 1905, and the 1930s were very warm. Focusing on just the past 60 years, the coldest decade on record was from 1975 to 1984. Since 2000 the average temperature has been around 50.6 degrees Fahrenheit, slightly higher than the long-term average. But with so much variation, it is too soon to be sure that a long-term change in average temperature is happening locally.

Precipitation and snowfall patterns have varied as well. Since 1965 annual precipitation has increased from a range of 28.7 to 34.7 inches to 32.5 to 38.2 inches. The wettest years on record in Toledo have occurred since 2005, and there does seem to have been an increase in extreme rain events in recent years. The snowiest decade on record was from 2005 to 2014, when annual average snowfall reached 44.9 inches. However, this number is strongly influenced by the record winter of 2013-14. Although records show that, on average, more snow has fallen in recent years, winter does seem to be getting shorter. From 1965 to 1994 the average number of days between the last snow of spring and the first snow of fall was 218. But since the mid-1990s the average has increased to 244 days. Whatever the future brings, we can be sure that the weather will continue to exert a big influence on our lives.

CHAPTER TWO

Beneath Our Feet

In this chapter, we continue to describe the physical setting of Lucas County with three essays on the formation of the ground we walk on: The ancient bedrock that formed millions of years in the past, the glaciers that scoured across that bedrock thousands of years ago, and the soils that have formed since those glaciers retreated.

Underfoot in Lucas County: The Bedrock
By Dr. Mark Camp

When Ohio gained statehood in 1803, one of the first tasks assigned to the new state geological survey was to discover what useful geologic materials were hidden in its hills, swamps, forests, and prairies. Along the Maumee River and its tributaries, the earliest explorers got a glimpse of the min-

The Maumee river rapids near Roche de Bout and the interurban bridge. (Photo by Art Weber)

eral resources that would help foster development of this vast territory. Rocky rapids of the Maumee River, particularly just upstream from Maumee, at Waterville, and at the county border northeast of Grand Rapids, were well surveyed and became the first sources of rock in the county.

Early settlers pried slabs from the river bed to use in the construction of their cabins and barns. Quarries appeared, first in the river bed and floodplain, and later throughout the county where bedrock was close to the surface. Limestone at Whitehouse and Monclova became a favorite building material. A narrow band of sandstone near Sylvania was hoped to be good grindstone material for grist mills, but it was too crumbly. Even so, it was destined to play an important part in Toledo history—with the discovery of natural gas, the local glass industry began and found this sandstone perfect for its needs.

The production of lime became important as the forests were cleared, wetlands drained, and farming begun. The bedrock was found to be dominantly limestone and dolostone (a rock similar to limestone but formed in saltier water), most of which could be fired and turned into useful products. As the county became settled, crushed rock was needed for paving projects and in the manufacture of cement. Today, the small quarries of the past have become local ponds and swimming establishments, or they have been swallowed up by major quarrying operations that have opened large deep pits into the underlying bedrock.

The eastern part of Lucas County is underlain by dolostones, formed around 430 million years ago. Under downtown Toledo, Adams and Washington Townships, southwest to Maumee and Waterville, and east of the Maumee River, the rock represents ancient deposition in a shallow equatorial sea, some 100 to 200 feet deep. Reefs formed in these warm shallow seas and were the home of many ancient creatures, including corals, sponges, bryozoans, brachiopods, crinoids, snails and clams, large animals

A trilobite.
(From the collection of Gene Roe)

A pair of blastoids (above) and a cluster of brachiopods (right).

with cone-shaped shells called nautiloids, sea scorpions, trilobites, early fish, algae, and many other creatures, all of which can now be found as fossils.

Up the Maumee River at Maumee, the rocks are slightly younger, around 425 million years old, and formed when the county was tidal flats periodically covered with water. Compared to the reef, this environment was very harsh and home to a much smaller population of organisms; thus, fossils are uncommon. The exceptions are the large mound-like growths of fossil cyanobacteria and algae that now dot the bedrock flats at Side Cut Metropark. Even younger dolostones form bedrock flats at Farnsworth Metropark at Waterville. As sea level continued to lower, the remaining water became very

salty, leading to the growth of minerals like gypsum and halite (common salt) as the water evaporated. To the east, in neighboring Ottawa County, these evaporites have been exposed in quarries and mines near Gypsum, Ohio.

About 416 million years ago, the county was again covered by a shallow sea. Evidence of this sea can be found in townships in western Lucas County. Here several dolostones, sandstones, limestones, and shale occur, but their occurrence at the surface is limited to a number of north-south trending bands roughly paralleling the border between Fulton and Lucas Counties. The rock layers decrease in age as you move from east to west across the county, from around 420 million years old in the east to about 370

million in the west. Included among these layers is a fossil-rich limestone and shale, known throughout the world for its well-preserved fossils of trilobites, brachiopods, bryozoans, corals, crinoids, and many of the same creatures that inhabited the early reefs of this area. You can still collect these fossils at Sylvania Township's Fossil Park off Centennial Road.

The appearance of several outcrop bands in the western townships is due to a slight bend in the layers. The beds tilt westward at a slightly steeper angle on the west side of a large subsurface formation

known as the Findlay Arch. At times this arch was dry land, which led to the erosion of rock layers at its crest. Thus, rock layers found in western Lucas County match rock layers far to the east in Erie County. At Farnsworth Metropark in Waterville, the bedrock bears the marks of earthquake activity—the resulting Bowling Green Fault extends some 90 miles south, terminating in western Hancock County. Look for displaced layers of dolostone in the rocky bluffs opposite Roche de Bout, near the edge of the river.

Since about 365 million years ago, any younger

Facing page: the bedrock Side Cut Metropark riverine alvar. (Photo by Art Weber)

Left: Evidence of the Bowling Green Fault, visible at Farnsworth Metropark. (Photo by Art Weber)

rocks formed in what is now Lucas County have left no trace, since everything more recent was removed by advancing ice sheets. These mile-thick glaciers acted as gigantic bulldozers, stripping away any younger layers of rock and leaving telltale scratches (striations) and grooves on the dolostone bedrock. These striations can be readily seen at Blue Creek Conservation Area in Whitehouse.

Quaternary History of Lucas County
By Dr. Timothy Fisher

Sediment of varying thickness overlies the bedrock in Lucas County. The depth of the sediment layer varies from zero along the Maumee River rapids where the bedrock is exposed, to 115 feet deep in other parts of the county. The term sediment is a catch-all phrase for clay, silt, sand and gravel. All of it is here as a result of glaciers that advanced south from Canada a few dozen times in the past 2.6 million years.

The upper few feet of sediment that freeze and thaw each year, are host to a variety of organisms from bacteria to Woodchucks, and contain variable amounts of organic material, all of which form soil. The various types of soils are dependent upon the parent material they develop in, and the different parent materials make up the different landforms across Lucas County. While many consider the area to be flat, there are a great many different types of landforms that record the history of land-forming events that began during the last ice age, which began locally about 30,000 years ago.

Periodically, changes in the geometry of Earth's orbit around the sun and its rotation about its axis cause more snow to fall in northern Canada than melts each summer. As the snow accumulates more sunlight is reflected back into space, and the Earth slowly cools. Once the snow is thick enough it turns to ice, and when the ice is about 100 feet thick it slowly deforms at its base and starts sliding southward along a thin film of water. At this point the ice is called a glacier. During the Ice Age the glacier was three miles thick, and as it advanced southward much of the ice was funneled through the Great Lakes basins, sliding across present-day Lucas County before stopping just north of present-day Cincinnati. While the ice was sliding along it acted like sandpaper, scouring the bedrock and sediment, slowly eroding it away. Rocks embedded in the base of the glacier were dragged across the bedrock, generating scratches, or striations, that record the direction the glacier was traveling. Striations are observable at the east side of Fossil Park in Sylvania and in Whitehouse. In other cases, water trapped beneath the glacier is under such tremendous pressure that as it flows between the glacier and the bedrock, it scoured grooves into bedrock, such as at Kelleys Island in western Lake Erie.

With continued changes in Earth-Sun geometry, the climate begins to warm and more ice melts at the ice margin than comes forward each year to re-

Facing page: Glacial grooves on Kelleys Island. (Photo by Art Weber)

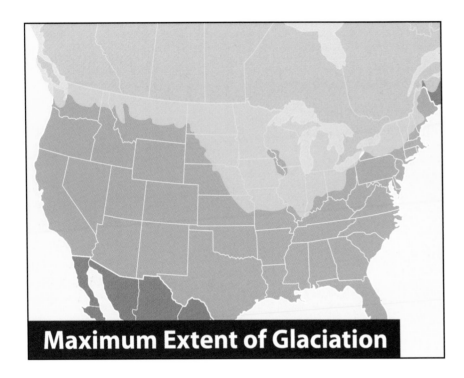

Maximum Extent of Glaciation

are left behind. But when the glacier retreats down a slope, the glacier is occupying the lowest elevations on the landscape, and dams the meltwater in front of the glacier, forming a lake. This is the situation when Lucas County was deglaciated, and the resulting lake was called Ancestral Lake Erie.

We know there was a lake here because at different elevations in the county are former beaches. The beaches are mostly composed of sand with some gravel and are very similar to the modern beaches around Lake Erie. The best-known beach of Ancestral Lake Erie is the Warren Beach, which is the large ridge of sand where the Oak Openings Region is located.

The sand of the Oak Openings Region in Lucas County is up to three miles wide and 42 feet deep. The ridge is a spit of land that was built by waves and currents about 14,500 years ago, when water was about 82 feet higher than the current lake level. After the lake level had dropped the climate became drier and windier.

Much of the Oak Openings ridge was reshaped by the wind forming thousands of small parabolic-shaped sand dunes ten to twenty feet high around 12,000 years ago. When the climate became warmer and wetter, the vegetation was able to stabilize the sand and the dunes have not been active since, except where the vegetation has been removed or disturbed, an example of which is the Girdham Road dunes in Oak Openings Preserve Metropark.

During deglaciation the rivers flowed into early high stages of ancestral Lake Erie. When the retreating glacier uncovered the Niagara River on the east-

place it. When this happens year after year, the glacier margin begins to retreat. Not as much erosion takes place during the glacial retreat, and sediment that had been eroded from further up the ice gets deposited beneath the glacier. Usually this sediment is not very well sorted and can range in size from clay to large boulders. This unsorted mix of sediment is called glacial till, and much of the surface sediment across Lucas County is till, which helps explain the region's clay-rich soils.

When the glacier retreats up a slope all of the meltwater flows away from the glacier. When this happens deposits of sand and gravel called outwash

Maple roots blow out at the Girdham Road sand dunes at Oak Openings Preserve Metropark.
(Photo by Art Weber)

ern edge of Lake Erie, the lake fell to about 100 feet below its current level. This is because the thickness of ice at the east end of the lake was greater than at the west end, so the Earth's crust was pushed down by the weight of the ice about 100 feet further than at the west end. Since then, with the weight of the ice removed, the outlet at the east end of Lake Erie has been rising (rebounding) at a faster rate than the west end, causing the lake level to rise at the western end by approximately 3.5 inches a century.

Between 12,000 and 6,500 years ago, Lake Erie did not receive any water from Lake Huron because Huron was draining out a northern outlet and did not switch to its current outlet at Port Huron, Michigan until about 6,500 years ago. During this time beaches formed in eastern Lake Erie at elevations well below the base of the Niagara River; in other words, for about 5,500 years Lake Erie had inflowing water but no outflowing water. With such fluctuations in lake level, the rivers had to adapt. Rivers generally cut downward, forming valleys when lake levels fall. This explains why the major rivers (Maumee River, Ottawa River, and Swan Creek) are all found within valleys. However, as lake levels rise, the lower part of the valley becomes submerged and the base of the valley fills with stream-deposited sediment. The Ottawa River valley is an estuary, or drowned river valley.

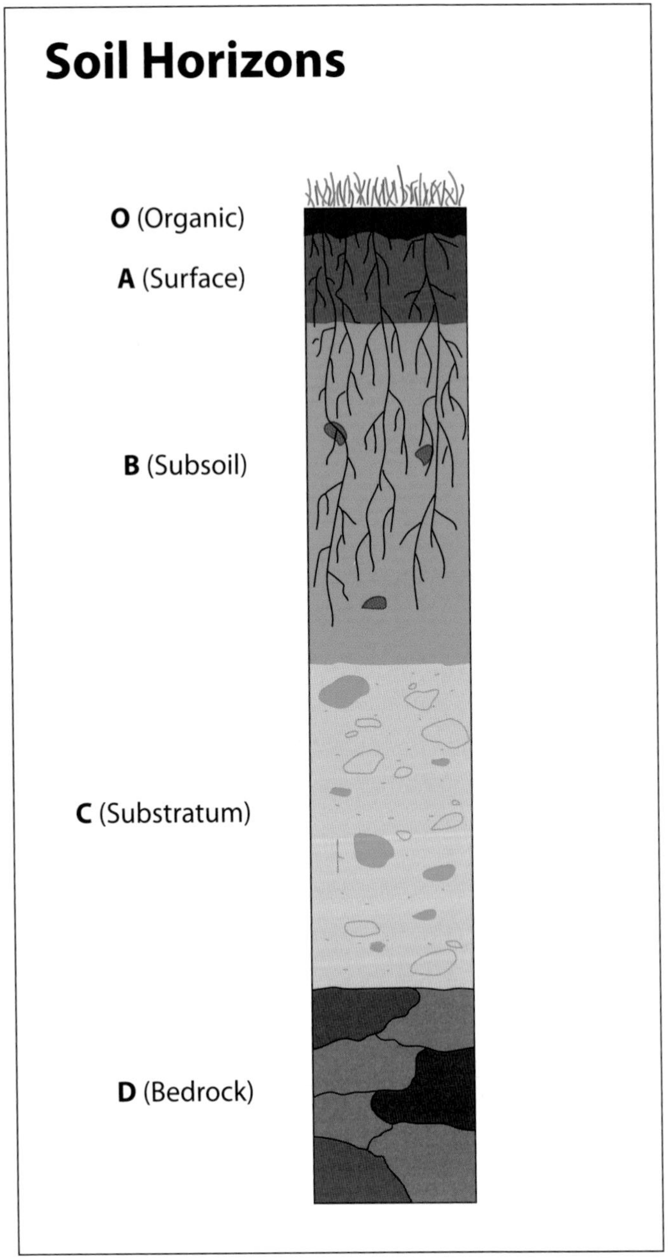

Soil Horizons

O (Organic)

A (Surface)

B (Subsoil)

C (Substratum)

D (Bedrock)

Lucas County Soils
By Matt Horvat

Soil is a complex mixture of minerals, liquids, dead organic matter, and gases that forms on the land surface. It usually has horizons, or layers, that are visible when a cross-section of soil is excavated. The sequence of layers is called a soil profile. The profile results from a combination of additions of litter and other materials on the surface, the activities of organisms living in the soil, the passage of water through the layers (upward or downward), and chemical reactions within the soil. The percentage of soil that is organic (composed of living and dead material) is generally highest at the surface.

Freezing and thawing, rainfall, and temperature all influence the development of a soil. Rainfall can leach (move) nutrients downward from the surface deeper into the soil and can even move fine clay particles downward. Plants, fungi, bacteria, and a host of small soil animals also work to develop soils by increasing the organic layer or by breaking down nutrient compounds.

The upper limit of soil is the boundary between soil and air. For submerged soils, the upper limit is the water, live plants, or dead plant material that has not begun to decompose. Submerged areas are not considered to have soil if the surface is permanently covered by water too deep (typically more than eight feet) for the growth of rooted plants. The lower boundary that separates soil from the nonsoil underneath is more difficult to define. Soil, in contrast to the underlying parent material, has been altered by the interactions of climate, relief, and living organisms over time. Commonly, the lower boundary is rock or hard materials virtually devoid of animals, roots, or other marks of biological activity. Soils vary in thickness; in some locations the soil may be very deep; in others soil may be absent and the bedrock is exposed at the surface.

The soil has a big impact on the development of an area and is one of the reasons that this part of northwest Ohio was among the last to be developed, since much of the area was low-lying and wet. Often, the soils that are higher and drier are settled and built upon first. You can see some evidence of this when you look out on an agricultural field; the farm woodlots were typically on the wettest soils and the hardest to drain. Generally, our soils are either clays formed on historical lake bottoms, or sandy soils on historic lake beaches such as the Oak Openings. The broad lake plain soils were so poorly drained that most of northwest Ohio was referred to as the Great Black Swamp. Trees adapted to wet conditions flourished and towered over the landscape concealing the deep sticky clay beneath, making travel by wagon nearly impossible. It wasn't until around 1850 that immigrants to the area began installing drainage tile to lower the water table and help dry the rich clay soils.

The eastern portions of Lucas County, including the City of Oregon and Jerusalem Township, have clay soils. Similar soils can be found in the northwest part of the county in Richfield Township and another small inclusion stretching parallel to the Maumee River from the City of Maumee to the Village of Waterville. These clay soils tend to be quite productive for agriculture if they are drained through subsurface drainage tiles.

The remainder of the soils in Lucas County, about 50 percent, are the sandy soils of the area known as the Oak Openings. These soils originated on beaches and beach ridges of the same lake that was responsible for the flat topography and heavy clay soils that lie to the east and northwest. The sandy soil stretches in a band running roughly northeast from Swanton through Sylvania into Michigan. The area can easily be seen on satellite and other aerial imagery as it shows up as being largely forested; the natural vegetation cover has been retained because the sandy soils have a high water table, are difficult to drain, and were terrible for farming. The beach ridges and sand dunes typically exist on a layer of dense, clay glacial till which serves to hold groundwater up above the bedrock.

Variations in depth of the water table have great effects on the soil and the vegetation that might grow on it. Low areas will have a very high water table and tend to accumulate organic matter, often appearing dark in color. Soils on higher ground or on top of ancient beach ridges will appear lighter and brighter in color as they are exposed to oxygen-containing air, which helps to quickly break down organic materials while precipitation also pulls the products of their decay (nutrients) deeper in the sandy soil.

CHAPTER THREE

History of Human Occupation

Native Americans: The Earliest Residents
By Eric Durbin

As the last glacial lakes drained away, the first people moved into northwest Ohio. The distinctive stone tools they left behind, particularly their robust spear points, identify them as big game hunters. Archeologists date finds of their tools to about 12,700 years ago. These were Ice Age men pursuing Ice Age megafauna—mastodon, bison, moose—through the muskeg and tundra that was the first landscape of Lucas County.

This chilly new "Eden" did not last long. The continuing retreat of the ice front, and a warming of the climate 8,000 to 10,000 years ago, replaced the harsher habitats with lush deciduous woodland

What was once the black swamp is now some of the region's best farmland. (Photo by Art Weber)

A fawn at Secor Metropark. (Photo by Art Weber)

(which still blanketed most of eastern North America when Europeans arrived). Simultaneously, the iconic Ice Age fauna disappeared from Ohio, presumably due in part to the depredations of the early Native Americans, and were supplanted by species with which we are more familiar—elk, whitetail deer, cougar, black bear, gray wolf, porcupine, raccoon, and, most fatefully because of the high value of its fur, the beaver.

Native Americans adapted their tool kit to match the changing fauna. An abundance of small arrow points in the archeological record testify to the bow's rise as the predominant weapon. Other common stone tools—scrapers and cutting edges—suggest the processing of meat and leather. Chert, the

raw material for making these sharp-edged stone tools, was quarried from the exposed bedrock in the Sylvania area, from the same locations as modern quarries. On March 27, 1969, members of the Toledo Area Aboriginal Research Club discovered more than 100 surviving native American quarry pits near Medusa Quarry. These small pits—four to six feet in diameter and one to two feet deep—pock the surface outcroppings where, using alternated fire and water to crack the encapsulating rock, chert nodules were dislodged and hauled away to worksites.

The hardwood forest provided wood for fuel and tools and bark for shelters and canoes, and its nut trees were a valuable food resource. Before the introduction of the European honey bee, the sap of maple trees, boiled into syrup, was the only abundant and reliable source of sweetener for Native Americans.

Finally, to their skills as hunters and gatherers, Native Americans added fishing and agriculture. Crops such as beans, squash, and maize were introduced by contact with peoples to the south, perhaps a thousand years ago, and universally adopted. As storing and preparing vegetable foods became important, clay pottery proliferated in the archeological record. The clay-rich soils laid down by the glaciers provided ample material for ceramic-making.

The banks of the Maumee and Ottawa Rivers and Swan Creek were particularly suited for farming, being better drained and having fewer mosquitoes than the surrounding swamp forests and wet prairies. In addition, during the growing season, the streams provided fishing opportunities to supplement the more sedentary, agricultural life style.

While adapting to living in northwest Ohio, Native Americans were unquestionably evolving culturally and politically. But as a people without written language, detailed information about Native American society for the thousands of years between their arrival and the arrival of the Europeans is lacking. Moreover, European trade goods, firearms, and diseases preceded as well as accompanied the Europeans, drastically altering whatever society had originally existed. Consequently, the descriptions of the Native American "tribes," their cultures and histo-

ries, and their relationships to each other, as recorded by those first Europeans, provide us only a blurry snapshot of what native society had been.

During the first half of the 1660s, the so-called Beaver Wars raged through New York and Pennsylvania, and then spread west to the Northwest Territory, which included present-day Lucas County. Iroquois-speaking tribes from the east, armed with guns received from Dutch and English traders, and bent upon seizing the lucrative beaver fur trade, descended upon and devastated the mainly Algonquin-speaking peoples of Ohio. Local tribes fled, were absorbed, or disappeared. Lucas County, like much of the state, was depopulated of its original inhabitants and essentially unpopulated by native

Re-enactors at Providence Metropark. (Photo by Art Weber)

peoples until the 1700s, when various tribes crept back into the vacuum that was northwest Ohio. These immigrant tribes are the ones that entered European literature and have dominated our view of our Native American past.

When General Anthony Wayne and his Legion arrived in 1794 to enforce the United States' claim on the Northwest Territory, in Lucas County he found and fought an assortment of newly-arrived tribes. The Potawatomi, while among the original residents encountered by the French, had fled north during the Beaver Wars and only recently returned. The Hurons (also called Wyandots), while Iroquoian speakers, had not been spared from the Iroquois onslaught, and had moved in from the east. The Shawnee, driven from their homelands in the east by different intertribal wars, had relocated to northwest Ohio in the 1700s.

The era of Native Americans ended in Ohio in the 1830s. A series of U.S. congressional acts authorized the forced removal of tribes throughout eastern United States from their ancestral homelands to federal reservations in the west.

Early European Settlement
By Dr. Larry Nelson

Americans knew very little about northwest Ohio prior to the War of 1812. Most associated the area with the Great Black Swamp, widely understood to be a nearly impenetrable morass extending some 40 miles north and south and 140 miles east and west laying along the southern border of the Maumee Valley. Because the area was both remote and believed to be uninhabitable and economically unviable, the federal government had ceded it to the Northwest Territory's Native peoples in the 1795 Treaty of Greenville. Only a small number of Europeans lived within the area, and beyond the Indian nations who called the Maumee Valley their home, few others had either the means or a reason to travel within the region.

Despite its isolation, the Maumee River was one of the most important rivers in northern Ohio. In the eighteenth and early nineteenth centuries, a time when water provided the only reliable means of transportation over long distances, the Maumee and its tributaries provided access into Ohio, Michigan, and the interior of Indiana. Further, travelers who followed the stream to its headwaters in present-day Fort Wayne, Indiana could then undertake a short portage to the Wabash River, which would carry them eventually to the Ohio and Mississippi Rivers. The Maumee rapids—a fourteen-mile series of shallow rapids extending from present-day Grand Rapids, Ohio to present-day Maumee and Perrysburg in which the river drops 55 feet—constituted only a modest obstacle to those moving along the stream. The Maumee River, therefore, formed a key element in a generally unimpeded transportation corridor extending from western New York and Pennsylvania all the way to the Gulf of Mexico. Early travelers used the river like modern drivers use interstate highways. They passed through the region, but rarely explored beyond the river's banks.

The onset of the War of 1812 focused enormous

public attention on the vicinity. Americans followed the events associated with Hull's Defeat, the Battle of the River Raisin, the first and second sieges of Fort Meigs, and the other military campaigns in northwest Ohio closely. The war also brought large numbers of people into the region for the first time. The personal observations of many of the soldiers who served in the area led them to recognize that the region possessed significant commercial potential despite its challenging topography and terrain.

The first detailed natural descriptions of the area were written during this time.

Soldiers were astonished by the region's beauty. One officer marching toward Detroit in 1812 remembered that his troops' first unexpected view of the "luxuriant" and "verdant" Maumee River as they emerged from the Black Swamp "enlivened the countenances of the fatigued soldiers and created joy and admiration throughout all the army." Another claimed that the region's exquisite scenery

Islands of Water Willow growing in the Maumee River rapids above Roche de Bout. (Photo by Art Weber)

could cause travelers to imagine that they had been "transported into the *Elysium* of the ancients." "The philosophic mind," he mused, "will rarely enjoy a richer feast than nature here presents."

As soldiers marched north from the Maumee, they encountered generally level terrain covered in hardwood forests consisting of hickories; white, black, and red oak; white and black walnut; American beech, ashes, black cherry, mulberry, honey-locust, poplars, and sugar maple. Nearer the lake, forests gave way to expansive plains, some of them many miles in extent, covered in summer in grass six to eight feet tall and a variety of colorful prairie flowers. The land bordering Lake Erie's western basin became gently rolling and covered in whortle-berry, cranberries, and small shrubs and underbrush down to the water's edge. The climate, noted one observer, was somewhat cooler than in southern Ohio, but the weather less changeable.

The soil within the region was a dark, loose, friable loam suitable for the production of corn, wheat, rye, oats, and barley. One traveler insisted that there was "probably not an acre of land within this territory but what may be cultivated to advantage." Native peoples living within the region had learned to expertly exploit the area's agricultural potential. General "Mad" Anthony Wayne was amazed at the scope and success of Indian agriculture as he marched toward Fallen Timbers in 1794, remarking that he had never seen such extensive fields of corn in any other part of America, "from Maine to Florida." And even though only a small number of Europeans lived along the lower Maumee Valley in 1812,

Lewis Bond, one of these early pioneers, reckoned the settlers living there were capable of producing "an immense quantity of corn, potatoes, oats, and wheat," while the surrounding forests supplied enough mast and forage to support "large droves of cattle and hogs."

Wildlife was abundant within the region. Early accounts speak of buffalo (bison), beaver, passenger pigeon, turkey, (whitetail) deer, elk, black bear, wildcat (bobcats and cougars) and (gray) wolf. One visitor asserted the region was "literally alive with creatures and beasts," but also plagued with mosquitoes and gnats.

Fish teemed in the Maumee River. Species including pike, pickerel, bass, sturgeon, sheepshead, and muskellunge inhabited the stream in great numbers. An officer serving at Fort Meigs (near present-day Perrysburg) in 1813 wrote "I took sail in a small canoe this morning and caught 62 white bass that would weigh about one pound each; caught them with a hook and line baited with a red rag." Another soldier remembered that "about the break of day myself and one more went to river to spear some fish. In the space of 30 minutes we had 67 fish which weighed from one to seven pounds. We caught them all by walking up the shore and plunging our spears in by random. Caught sometimes three and frequently two at a stroke." A third witnessed two or three others fill half a barrel with fish within a short time using only "clubs and stones" to secure their prey.

Other observers realized that the area's natural attributes would help propel future development.

Recognizing the potential power that could be generated by the water flowing through the rapids, and the fact that Maumee Bay provided a navigable harbor and access to Lake Erie, many predicted a time when the whole length of the lower-Maumee would be "lined with mills and other manufactories" and the mouth of the river would boast "as fine an inland town as any in the union."

Prior to European settlement, the Maumee Valley was a place abounding in wildlife, rich in natural resources, and possessing the qualities necessary for future development. The climate was hospitable and the soil fertile. Native peoples had demonstrated the region's capacity for agricultural production. Visitors were beginning to recognize that all of these attributes, when combined with the economic potential evinced by the Maumee rapids and Maumee Bay, could be powerful engines for economic growth. Yet, perhaps it was the area's beauty that most captivated those who traveled within the region. In March 1813, Capt. Daniel Cushing spent a few moments in quite reflection watching the Maumee River as it flowed past his post at Fort Meigs. "The river is gliding through the meadows swiftly and covered with all kinds of water fowl," he wrote, "and the ice which was left by the high water on the meadows is without bounds from three to fifteen feet deep, and that over more than half of the bottoms." "At this time," he claimed, "this is the most romantic looking place that ever my eyes saw. To look from the battery onto the river and meadows is the greatest charm of any place that ever was in any country that ever I traveled in."

The Great Black Swamp

When the first Europeans arrived in this area in the seventeenth century, they found a vast swamp lying like a moat across northwestern Ohio. The wettest section lay east of the Maumee River, encompassing present-day Wood, Seneca, Ottawa, and the eastern portion of Lucas counties. In early spring, the combination of snow melt and rain caused floods that spread out across the swamp. Drainage was so poor that the land often remained flooded well into summer, and even in other seasons the mud and mosquitoes made travel across the swamp extremely difficult. In the 1820s a road was constructed through the area, described at the

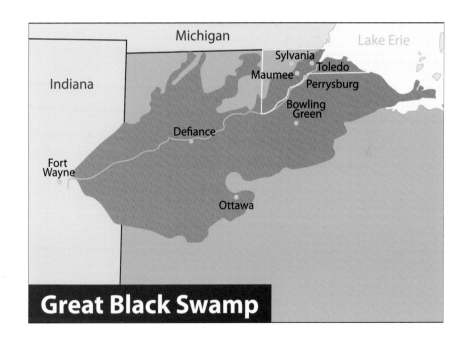

Great Black Swamp

time as the worst road on the North American continent. Wagons often became stuck in the deep mud, and progress was so slow that inns were built every mile along the way so that travelers could find lodging each night.

Early accounts of the Black Swamp describe stands of towering trees whose dense foliage shut out much of the sunlight during the warmer months.

Dominant trees in the swamp included silver maple, cottonwood, American elm, and green and black ash. Where drainage was better—on banks at the river's edge, and on slightly higher ground—common trees included sycamore, Ohio buckeye, black walnut, and honeylocust.

Relatively few herbaceous plants could cope with the heavy shade under the dense canopy, but

This scene from Secor Metropark is how the Black Swamp may have appeared to early settlers to the region. (Photo by Art Weber)

where treefalls provided light gaps, the fertile soils and abundant moisture allowed for rapid growth. We occasionally see this response today along Swan and Tenmile Creeks, where in a single summer, dense stands of giant ragweed, cutleaf coneflower, wingstem, stinging nettles, and a few other flood-tolerant species grow to heights of six feet or more in floodplain openings.

Much early settlement occurred west of the river, where the land was less swampy. In the1830s a barge canal along the west bank of the Maumee allowed goods to be moved up and down the river, circumventing the rapids. The Anthony Wayne Trail (the present-day U.S. Route 24) occupies a portion of the bed of the old canal. Remnants of the canal locks are preserved at Side Cut and Providence Metroparks and a few other locations.

The Black Swamp itself was not tamed until tile drainage techniques were widely adopted after the Civil War. Then, drainage and forest clearance occurred very rapidly, so that by the 1880s the swamp was essentially gone, the ancient trees converted to building materials, and the land planted in crops. Today the former swamp lands are fields of corn, soybeans, and wheat, and it is difficult to believe a swamp forest ever existed there.

The locks at Providence Metropark, near Grand Rapids, with three modes of transportation: boats, trains, and trucks. Canals and their accompanying boats were subsequently replaced by trains, and the advent of semi trucks and a national highway system had a big impact on the rail industry. (Photo by Art Weber)

The Modern Era

Deforestation was by far the most powerful agent of change wrought by Europeans; by the end of the nineteenth century less than ten percent of Lucas County remained in forest cover. But profound changes in the area's landscape did not end with the clearing of the forest; change has continued right up to the present day and will continue for the foreseeable future.

Coupled with the removal of the forest, the construction of ditches, tile drains, and the more recent practices of stream clearance and channelization have combined to alter our water regime. These changes were designed to speed the runoff of water so that fields—many of them on former swamp land with water tables near the surface—would be dry enough to farm. The surging runoff eroded stream banks, incised (cut deeper) stream beds, and carried topsoil from the fields downstream. Quickly, the aquatic meadows of wild rice that covered Maumee Bay in pioneer days were suffocated by silt that smothered the seed bank and blocked the sunlight needed for the young plants to grow beneath the water. Waterways that had run clear when the pioneers arrived became cloudy with suspended soil particles.

Rapid industrial growth began in the late 1800s. The Lake Erie shore had no coal, oil, or iron ore, but was strategically located between huge deposits of all three. Iron ore was shipped down from Minnesota, and oil wells and coal fields existed to the east in Pennsylvania. What we did have was abundant fresh water, needed for heavy industry. Simultaneously, the development of railroads and the construction of locks on the Great Lakes facilitated rapid transport of raw materials to factories along Lake Erie. Toledo expanded rapidly. By the 1890s it was second only to Cleveland as an oil refining center. The Libbey Glass Company came to Toledo in 1888 from Massachusetts, lured by the sand deposits and cheap fuels, and the discovery of abundant natural gas at Findlay, just 40 miles south of Toledo. Industry meant jobs, so people surged into northern Ohio. The population of the Lake Erie basin soared from three million in 1900 to fifteen million by 1980.

Farming also was changing. In 1900 the average farm was only about 100 acres. Fields were small and bordered by brushy fencerows or hedges that provided wildlife cover and windbreaks. Crops were rotated and land was often "rested" for a year, or cycled between crops and pasture. Manure and legumes were plowed under to maintain soil fertility, and farmers grew much of what they consumed at their own tables.

After 1920, however, the advent of motorized farm machinery made it more economical to grow monocultures on much larger fields. Farmers grew one or two cash crops and kept little or none of what they grew, buying most of their food from the store, like city dwellers. Hedgerows were cleared away, reducing wildlife cover and accelerating the erosion of topsoil. The almost universal use of synthetic fertilizers and chemical pesticides after 1945 promoted even larger monocultures and caused further degradation of water quality.

Since the late twentieth century, the most profound environmental change has been the rapid expansion of building across the county. As mentioned in Chapter 1, Lucas County has been gradually losing population since 1970, but the expansion of shopping malls, commercial strip developments, and residential subdivisions has continued at a rapid pace. Virtually all of this expansion has been onto former farmland.

Despite these trends, there has been a net increase in forest cover in recent years as farmland on poor soils—mostly in the Oak Openings—has been abandoned. Many of the farms failed during the dry, hot years of the Great Depression (1930s);

others were abandoned after World War II as the sons and daughters of farm families sought jobs in the city. The result has been the formation of extensive tracts of second-growth forest across portions of western Lucas County. Much of this land has been incorporated into protected areas by Metroparks Toledo, The Nature Conservancy, and various state agencies. Along the Lake Erie shore, thousands of acres of wetland have been restored and protected by the combined efforts of private landowners and federal and state wildlife agencies. These hopeful trends suggest that our landscape will continue to provide abundant open space for both human recreational needs and wildlife.

Corn awaiting harvest on a modern farm. (Photo by Art Weber)

CHAPTER FOUR

Plants Across the County

Lucas County, with its moist temperate climate, has abundant plant life. We tend to take that for granted, but visitors to Ohio from the dry western states often comment on the lush appearance of our landscape. In this chapter, we introduce some of the common, widespread plants you are most likely to see as you drive about the county. Lucas County is also known for its rare and endangered plants— more than in any other Ohio county. Some of these special species will be treated later, mostly in Chapter 6 on the Oak Openings.

Plants may be divided into four categories according to their life histories:

Winter annuals germinate in late summer or fall, grow a small cluster of leaves, and then overwinter as a "rosette," a circular clump of leaves flattened to the ground beneath the snow. When warm weather

A large black oak in the front meadow at Wildwood Preserve Metropark. (Photo by Art Weber)

returns in spring they grow upward quickly, flower, produce seed, and die. Many small members of the mustard family that invade crop fields are winter annuals.

Summer annuals are not frost-hardy. They germinate in spring, grow quickly, flower, produce seed, and die all in one growing season. Common ragweed is one example; so are the colorful annuals we plant in our flower gardens, as well as many of our crops.

Biennials live more than one year, but flower only once. They spend a year or more producing leaves and root systems. Once they have stored enough energy in leaves and roots they bolt upward, produce flowers and seeds, and then die. Wild Carrot ("Queen-Anne's Lace") is a common biennial.

Perennials live for more than a year and can flower repeatedly. They may live and produce seeds for a very long time – hundreds of years, in the case of some trees. All woody plants are perennials, as well as some herbaceous plants, for example, most of our woodland wildflowers.

Trees

With the draining of the Great Black Swamp and the clearing of the forest, the land became much drier. Today most of the former swampland is in agriculture, and the farm woodlots—all second growth—are as likely to be dominated by oaks and hickories as by the trees that characterized the swamp. Close to 100 species of woody plants grow naturally here, as well as many introduced species. This section covers just a few of the most abundant ones.

Cottonwood may be the most widespread tree in the county. This tall, fast-growing tree thrives in moist soils, but may be seen almost anywhere except inside deep forests. It is most conspicuous in late May when it sheds its abundant fluffy white seeds; it is possible that every acre of land in the county receives at least a few wind-blown cotton-

Cottonwood leaves and some of its white fluffy seeds that are very prevalent in Lucas county. (Photo by Art Weber)

wood seeds each spring. Close inspection reveals that cottonwood trees, like humans, have separate sexes.

Male cottonwoods flower a bit earlier than the females; they produce chain-like strings of reddish flowers. Only the females produce the fluffy seeds; their flower strings are yellowish-green.

Oaks may outnumber all other trees here, although several species are involved. Oaks are most obvious from late October into mid-November, because they hold their leaves longer in the fall than most other native trees. They are relatively slow-growing and long-lived, and can achieve very large size. Their acorns provide an important food source for many wildlife species. Black oaks thrive on relatively sterile dry sandy soils and are the dominant tree in oak savannas of the Oak Openings of western Lucas County (although tree experts find that these trees are mostly hybrids of black oaks with other, related species).

At the other extreme, pin oaks can grow with their "feet" wet in seasonally flooded low areas. Bur oaks are common floodplain trees, although they do not fare well in standing water. White oaks are probably the most widespread species, growing in both dry and moist soils. A few very old white oaks may be seen along Indian Road in the village of Ottawa Hills.

"Mast-fruiting" is an interesting feature of oaks: A grove of oaks may produce extremely heavy acorn crops in one year and virtually none the next. One theory is that mast-fruiting is an adaptation that limits the consumption of acorns by insects, birds and

Red oak leaf and acorns. (Photo by Art Weber)

mammals. That is, if more acorns than animals can possibly eat are produced in one year, some acorns will survive to germinate. Then, by failing to produce acorns the next year, the tree essentially "starves out" acorn-eating animals, who then must move elsewhere for food. This prevents acorn-eaters from building up large populations in oak groves. Studies

are underway to determine whether Red-headed Woodpeckers in the Oak Openings are dependent on acorns to stay through the winter. Many of them stay over in some years, but in other years most of them depart, usually during October. Do the departure years conform to acorn-crop failures?

Floodplains along Swan Creek and the Ottawa River system probably best reflect the tree species composition of the former Black Swamp. Dominant trees include silver maple, cottonwood, honeylocust, black walnut, American sycamore, and, until the arrivals of Dutch elm disease and the Emerald Ash Borer, American elm and black and green ash.

Suburban streets throughout the county often have a diverse mix of planted shade trees, many of them native species. In the 1940s, thousands of fast-growing silver maples were planted on suburban tree lawns across our region. Unfortunately, old silver maples are fragile and potentially hazardous. Many have come down or shed massive branches in windstorms. Although old silver maples still line many streets, most communities have stopped planting them. Today, frequently-planted street trees include honey locust, sugar and red maples, various oaks, non-natives Norway maple and London Plane, and both native and non-native lindens.

Facing page: Part of the pine forest planted at Oak Openings Preserve Metropark in the 1940s. Many of these stands of non-native trees have reached their life expectancy and are being thinned or cleared entirely. (Photo by Art Weber)

The unfortunate loss of most of our American elms and ashes emphasizes the importance of planting a diversity of species. The elms succumbed in the 1960s to Dutch elm disease, caused by an introduced fungus spread from tree to tree by a bark beetle. The Emerald Ash Borer is a more recent invader from China, which rapidly moved across Lucas County in the early 2000s, killing virtually every ash tree more than three inches in diameter. Standing dead ashes still may be seen in many places, identifiable by their straight, stiff, slightly ascending twigs.

In the 1980s the University of Toledo planted dozens of ashes on its campus; all were lost when the borer arrived twenty years later. Monocultures (large stands of a single species) are rare in nature, because they are not adaptive; they can be easily wiped out by diseases or pests. We are learning—sometimes the hard way—that a landscape with a diverse mixture of species is more stable and, in the long run, less expensive to maintain, than a monoculture. More on the issue of invasive species appears in Chapter 9.

Cone-bearing evergreens such as spruces, hemlocks, and pines are frequent components of yard plantings. Since they seem to grow well in our area, it may surprise the reader to learn that no cone-bearing trees are native to Lucas County. The nearest natural populations occur not far away in Michigan, but when the first Europeans arrived none were here. Thus, all our cone-bearing evergreens are planted or are the descendants of planted trees, including the pine and spruce stands in Oak Openings Preserve Metropark and Maumee State Forest.

Agricultural Crops

About 35 percent of the land surface in Lucas County is devoted to agriculture. All but a tiny fraction of that farmland is in three crops: corn, winter wheat, and soybeans. These crops are annuals and must be replanted every year. It is interesting to note that as recently as 75 years ago agricultural practices here were somewhat different. Cover crops such as hay and alfalfa were grown frequently, and fields usually were not plowed all the way to the roadsides and ditch edges, as they are today. Fields were smaller; there were hedgerows and treelines that provided windbreaks and cover for wildlife, and fields were often allowed to lay fallow for a year. Beginning in the 1940s the development of synthetic chemical pesticides and fertilizers and hybrid crop strains has allowed farmers to grow large monocultures, and the economics of modern agriculture have dictated that as much acreage as possible be kept in continuous production. Large combines used to harvest corn leave a lot of grain in the field, so corn stubble fields do provide a resource for wildlife in fall and winter. However, fields of wheat and soybeans have almost no value for wildlife.

One significant change is a trend toward less plowing. Formerly, fields were deep-plowed every fall and often again in spring. Some farmers have gone to no-till or reduced tillage methods, where last year's crop remains are left standing and a new crop planted amongst the stubble. This trend reduces the need for fertilizer and reduces soil loss to ditches and streams, although it may require the use of more herbicides to deter the growth of weeds. It also appears that not tilling keeps phosphorus near the soil surface, where it is more likely to be transported into streams. More about phosphorus as a pollutant appears in Chapter 9.

Unfortunately, our farms are fast disappearing. In the past 50 years a sizeable percentage of Lucas County's farm land has been converted to industrial parks, commercial strips, malls and housing subdivisions, and this trend continues.

Roadsides and Successional Habitats

Roadsides have their own specialized plant communities. Typically, roadside plants are adapted to harsh conditions including full sun, gravelly infertile soil, mowing, salt runoff from winter road deicing, exposure to wind, and extremes of temperature. Many roadside plants are considered to be "weeds." They readily invade farm fields and lawns if allowed to do so—something every homeowner notices when the dandelions bloom.

Probably at least 95 percent of our common roadside plants are native to Europe and were brought to our country unknowingly by the earliest European settlers. How did this happen? "Weeds" typically produce large numbers of small seeds that are easily dispersed across the landscape. Some, like the dandelions and thistles, are wind-dispersed. Others have sticky or fuzzy seeds that catch in the fur of mammals (or our pants legs) and are carried to new locations, where they are dropped when the animal cleans its fur. Some simply produce immense numbers of seeds with no obvious dispersal adaptations. The huge numbers of seeds and their small size made it easy for them to stow away in grain or other materials that were brought over when the first ships arrived from Europe. Also, despite their small size, some "weed" seeds can survive for many years, breaking dormancy only when conditions for germination are satisfied.

As you travel across the county, you will notice seasonal changes in the plants growing on the roadside. In spring, the yellow of dandelions and mustards predominates. In summer, they give way to the

The seed head of Goats Beard (above) along the Wabash Cannonball Trail and a swamp thistle at Wiregrass Lake Metropark (right). (Photo by Art Weber)

pale blue of chicory and the flat-topped white heads of Queen-Anne's lace, accompanied by squirrel-tail barley, a low grass whose tops look like shaggy brushes that ripple in the wind. In fall, yellow, white and purple dominate as members of the aster family take over.

Ecological succession is the process by which one plant community replaces another on land that is not being managed by humans. The sequence of plant communities that occurs at a given site in a given region is fairly predictable. In Lucas County, if a farm field is abandoned, the early years of succession are dominated by annuals and biennials whose seeds may have been lying in the soil for many years, waiting for conditions to be right for germination. Common plants in these early years include winter annuals of the mustard family, summer annuals such as common ragweed, and biennial thistles and sweet clovers. Later, biennial Queen-Anne's lace and herbaceous perennials gradually take over. Among those perennials are the goldenrods, whose blossoms fill our fallow fields with yellow from late August into October. Because goldenrods bloom when people are suffering from allergies caused by ragweed pollen, many mistakenly believe that goldenrods are ragweeds. They are not. In some fields, asters, ironweeds and Joe-pye-weed add touches of

Left: Coneflower and Queen Anne's Lace at Blue Creek Metropark. (Photo by Art Weber)

Facing page: A field of Canada Goldenrod at Swan Creek Preserve Metropark. (Photo by Art Weber)

white and purple to the goldenrod display.

Early in succession, birds visit the fields and bring the seeds of woody plants in their droppings. Other tree seeds (e.g., cottonwoods and sycamores) are blown in by the wind. Careful observation of the ground beneath the goldenrods may reveal the seedlings of shrubs and trees that will ultimately overtop and shade out the herbaceous plants. Thus, if left alone long enough, the abandoned field returns to forest. In Lucas County, it takes about 60 years for an abandoned field to return to a tall-canopied forest.

Common Woodland Wildflowers and Ferns

Spring is the best time for woodland wildflowers. Most of them emerge and flower early, gathering light energy needed for photosynthesis before the tree canopy leafs out overhead. First to emerge in March is the skunk cabbage, which grows abundantly wherever the soil is wet. Look for its maroon-tinted "hoods" poking up through the leaf litter in low places and along ravine seeps. Often hikers are aware of its presence before they see it, due

Trillium (right) at Secor Metropark, and skunk cabbage (far right) in a slough at Oak Openings Metropark. (Photos by Art Weber)

A stand of Mayapple clones at Secor Metropark.
(Photo by Art Weber)

to its rank odor. Common spring wildflowers include spring cress, hepatica, bloodroot and yellow trout lily in April, followed in May by trilliums, Mayapple, wild ginger, and in wet places, marsh marigold. Later in May, forest edges in the Oak Openings sport the bright yellow flowers of golden ragwort, and a few spots still support relict stands of yellow ladies-slipper orchids.

The Mayapple is one of our most familiar woodland plants, because its umbrella-like leaves often cover large areas of the forest floor from May through August. Some Mayapple plants have only a single leaf; others have two. Only the two-leaf plants produce flowers. A small percentage of the flowers produce fruits, which ripen in July. All parts of the plant are toxic except for the ripe fruits. These only last a few days before they are consumed by mice, box turtles, and beetles. Mayapple has a fascinating life history. Stands of Mayapple are often clones, formed over many years by the gradual vegetative spread of a single plant. Each green shoot grows at the end of a shallow pencil-thick rhizome. If a rhizome is dug up, you will see that it has a series of root-bearing nodes marking the locations where shoots had been produced in previous years. The sexual history of the plant can be estimated by measuring the length of each rhizome internode; when a long segment is produced, the plant is more likely to produce two leaves (and thus a flower) the following year. Occasionally a rhizome forks; when this happens each branch of the rhizome produces a shoot. After six to eight years, the old end of the rhizome— the end farthest from the shoot—will decay. In this way, plants that have forked will eventually become separated. As this process continues over many years, large clones of Mayapples can be produced.

In late summer and fall, woodland wildflower diversity is typically low and the flowers are small and unspectacular. A few species of aster and goldenrod may be found, along with enchanter's nightshade and Virginia smartweed. Along the Maumee River towpath, White snakeroot is often abundant at this season, joined in sunnier spots by Joepye-weed, ironweed, and additional goldenrods.

Ferns may be abundant in moist old-growth woodlots but are largely absent from young forest

Cinnamon fern and skunk cabbage near Mallard Lake at Oak Openings Preserve Metropark.
(Photo by Art Weber)

stands. The Oak Openings is an excellent place to see a half dozen of our commoner species. Dominating the ground cover in open oak savannas is the bracken fern, whose large triangular fronds may exceed three feet in height. In moister, shadier situations, tall cinnamon and interrupted ferns often grow together. Two other species are often present nearby, royal fern and sensitive fern, whose spore cases look like dry bunches of grapes at the tip of vertical stalks that persist long after the fronds have died away. More on ferns is included in Chapter 6.

Small Plants: Mosses, Lichens, Liverworts and Hornworts

By Janet Traub and James Toppin

Small plants live in worlds a few inches in size, where the weather and daylight may be much different from what we experience. The temperature of exposed surfaces such as bare sand, rock and roof shingles seesaws from hot and dry under the midday sun to cold and moist during the night. On the other hand, mosses and liverworts on an old log in deep woods grow in a dim, moist environment where temperature swings are not so dramatic. Treetop branches, where some lichens live, provide a much different environment from what we experience on the ground below. Rainwater running down a tree trunk, gathering particles of dust and organic matter on the way, may pool in knotholes or bring extra nutrients to niches at the tree base. In fact, the outdoors is really a mosaic of innumerable small and diverse worlds inhabited by mosses, lichens, liv-

Sensitive fern at Oak Openings Preserve Metropark.
(Photo by Christine Manzey)

erworts and hornworts. Since they are adapted to broad fluctuations in their environments, most of these tiny plants thrive year-round. We can enjoy their diversity regardless of the season.

Being so small, these plants do not need some of the structures that larger plants have for water transport, support and other functions. For example, they do not have roots; instead they absorb water and nutrients directly from the environment through their cell walls. The peat mosses (*Sphagnum*) have branch and leaf structures that conduct and hold water, allowing them to shape their own

boggy environment by keeping it wet and acidic, hindering the growth of trees that could shade them out.

There are over 100 kinds of mosses in Lucas County, and more than 400 kinds in Ohio. Several species live in our hottest, driest places—on bare exposed sand, rock or roof shingles—while one kind of moss, *Fissidens fontanus*, lives underwater, attached to rocks in streams: Swan Creek, for example. Mosses do not produce seeds. Instead, they release spores tiny enough to be carried by the wind. If the spores land in a favorable place, they germinate and produce new plants. Mosses can also spread if some part of the plant breaks off and ends up in a favorable place for it to grow into a new plant.

At a certain stage in their life cycle, mosses produce small brown capsules—less than 1/4-inch long—at the end of a short brown stalk growing off of the green moss plant. This capsule contains the spores. A very close look at the end of the capsule with a hand lens reveals one of the most fascinating structures in the plant world: a set of teeth, called the peristome, that flexes and straightens with changes in humidity, gradually releasing the spores from the capsule during favorable conditions. The teeth are typically reddish-brown tapering to a clear tip, with a beautifully detailed structure like a pale stained-glass window. Any time of year, one species or another will be bearing its capsules.

British Soldier lichen at the Girdham Road sand dunes at Oak Openings Preserve Metropark. (Photo by Art Weber)

Lichens are plants only in the broadest sense; they actually consist of a fungus that encloses algae or cyanobacteria (sometimes both). They inhabit the same kinds of small worlds that mosses do, although most lichens prefer sunny places. Many lichens are a shade of gray or off-green, but others are yellow, orange, brown or red. Some kinds grow as flat lobes forming patches, which are sometimes target shaped, up to several inches wide, while others take the form of stalks, cups, ox horns, branched masses or other shapes that pictures can demonstrate better than words.

Still other kinds grow on rocks as thin crusts that, because the lower part of the lichen actually grows into the rock, can only be removed by taking part of the rock too. Although lichens are extremely hardy and well adapted to harsh climates, many kinds are acutely sensitive to air pollution. As a result, some of the most sensitive lichens have become scarce in Ohio or are no longer found here, although populations of certain affected species have recovered in recent years as a result of regulations to reduce pollution.

You may notice large patches of gray or yellowish green "shield lichens" growing on tree trunks. Look also for the red-topped grayish-green stalks of the British soldier lichen growing on old wood or on soil. There, you also may see "pixie-cups," which are closely related to the British soldier, but instead of the red top have a funnel-shaped cup. In all, about 40 kinds of lichens have been found in Lucas County, and further searching will probably turn up more.

Liverworts resemble mosses in that they produce spores rather than seeds, but their spore capsules, which appear in spring, are more fragile and fleshier and wither after only a few days, unlike moss capsules, which may persist for weeks or even months. Some liverwort capsules look like tiny umbrellas. Unlike mosses, liverworts have obvious top and bottom surfaces. Liverworts have the distinction of being the oldest known land plants, with a fossil record dating back more than 460 million years. The greatest diversity of liverworts is in the tropics, although there are probably fifteen to twenty kinds in Lucas County.

One of the most noticeable liverworts in our area, although one of the smallest, is *Frullania eboracensis*. Look for very fine purple threads growing on tree trunks, especially visible on oaks with light-colored bark. A closer look reveals that the threads are stems with minute leaves (about 1/100-inch long). After seeing it for the first time, you will begin to notice that it is common in wooded areas, not only here but throughout Ohio and Michigan. Despite this, most people have never seen it.

Hornworts are the most elusive of our small plants. Like mosses and liverworts, hornworts produce spores, but the plant is a flat lobe or pancake with a horn-shaped stalk growing up out of the center of the lobe. This stalk is the spore capsule. Hornworts are primarily tropical plants—there are only a few species in Ohio. Look for them on bare disturbed soil (such as at the edges of farm fields) from late fall through winter until early spring, by which time they will have released their spores, which will germinate in fall to begin the next cycle.

Fungi

By Kim High

They exist nearly everywhere in the world and are essential to life as we know it, yet fungi are frequently overlooked, misunderstood, and underappreciated. In fact, our human interests are often associated with our stomachs or our immediate health, so that the most common questions about fungi become, "Can we eat it" or "Will it hurt me?" This discussion will address these questions somewhat, but the kingdom of fungi deserves regard and respect for other equally important reasons.

With estimates of 144,000 known species and probably well over a million yet to be described, fungi form an entire taxonomic Kingdom of their own. It wasn't too long ago that fungi were considered a part of the plant kingdom. But recent research shows that most fungal organisms function more like animals than plants. In most cases, they use enzymes to absorb and consume their nutrition from other organisms, rather than producing their own food from sunlight. Like some animal parasites, they live within their food sources. The fruiting bodies (mushrooms) that we see are only the reproductive parts of otherwise cryptic organisms entwined within the decaying earth, tree, soil, animal carcass, or other source of the fungi's sustenance. When conditions are right, such as after a heavy rain, those mushrooms release spores that disperse the genetic make-up of the parent fungus to new places, perpetuating its existence.

From the late twentieth century until now, not only the fungi kingdom but also its constituent taxonomic categories—phylum, class, order, family, genus and species—have been and continue to be reorganized dramatically as new evidence emerges about the molecular and evolutionary relationships of members of this fascinating group. Such systematic restructuring does not reflect easily visible differences. Thirty years ago, it would have been safe to say that the typical mushroom probably belonged to a group collectively called the Agarics, because they were in the historic taxonomic order, Agaricales. Today, gilled mushrooms and their relatives make up many orders, not just Agaricales, and mushrooms that don't look typical at all, such as the locally common giant puffball (*Calvatia gigantea*), have been moved to Agaricales. Some other groups of local mushrooms that have been moved to new Orders include the russalas, chanterelles, boletes, and polypores. These changes result in obsolete field guides, leading mushroom enthusiasts to cross reference their specimens via on-line identification tools. However, the out-of-date books still can be very useful for understanding general mushroom structure, location and growth habits.

For better or for worse, fungi impact the habitat in which they live. Beneficially, many serve as essential decomposers of organic material. Without saprophytic fungi, dead organisms likely would not break down, and the world as we know it could not exist. Also extremely valuable are the mycorrhizal relationships that certain fungi have with most plants. Contrary to popular belief, most fungi do not kill trees, but in fact function symbiotically. Fungi living in plants' roots offer plants added moisture and nutrients, while the plants in return provide the fungi with foods which they have produced through photosynthesis. Such symbiotic relationships between fungi and plants are considered essential for the success of many plant communities. More indirectly but critical to human health, fungi have provided the substances for penicillin and other life-saving antibiotics. Even some of the most locally common ones, such as turkey-tail fungus (*Trametes versicolor*), have been used medicinally by herbalists for centuries, to fight viruses and cancers.

One the other hand, some fungi are notably pathogenic. The culprits of highly destructive tree diseases like Dutch elm, chestnut blight and oak wilt are all fungi. So are many that cause serious infectious diseases in animals, such as the amphibian chytrid, *Batrachochytrium dendrobatidis*, and *Pseudogymnoascus destructans*, the cause of the lethal white-nose syndrome in bats. Currently, another often-fatal fungal disease has begun spreading among snakes in our region. Certain fungal spores and byproducts are agents of toxins and carcinogens that can wreak havoc on the health of many animal species, including humans, and some mushrooms common to Lucas County can be deadly to humans when ingested. Thus, considering the monumental impacts that fungi have on the welfare of our world, research and study surrounding the members of this

Turkey tail fungus on a downed log at Secor Metropark. (Photo by Art Weber)

diverse kingdom are paramount to our understanding of the environment.

Yet despite the incredible diversity in this kingdom, the word fungus generally conjures up a singular image of what most people commonly call a "mushroom." The remainder of this discussion will focus on the identification of these more typical fungi, especially in reference to some that are common here in Lucas County. Taxonomically, the typical mushroom is categorized in the phylum Basidiomycota, determined by the microscopic, internal structure and club-like shape of the organism's spore-producing cells, called sporangia. One exception is the famous edible morel (*Morchella esculentoides*) and its relatives, which are in the phylum Ascomycota, and microscopically have sac-like sporangia.

To figure out a mushroom's identity, one must look closely at several very specific characteristics. The presence of gills, pores, or teeth on the underside of the mushroom's cap, whether the gills are attached to the stem, the presence of a ring or annulus on the stem, the presence of cup or volva at the stem's base, and the color of the mushroom's spores all are critical identification characteristics. All these characteristics can be observed immediately except for the color of the spores, which is

Left: A morel mushroom at Swan Creek Metropark. (Photo by Art Weber)

Facing page: From left, fly amanita, shaggy mane, and destroying angel (poisonous). (Photos by Art Weber)

determined by taking a spore print. To take a spore print, neatly slice the mushroom's cap from its stem, lay the cap on a piece of white cardboard, and leave it lightly covered and undisturbed for about 12 to 24 hours. The mushroom's spores will drop onto the cardboard, leaving a design and revealing the spore color.

Sometimes a difference of just one of these characteristics separates species, genera and even families, and such distinctions can be matters of life and death if the observer is inclined to eat a mushroom gathered from the wild. A comparison of two mushroom families that are commonly seen in Lucas County lawns and woodlands demonstrates this point well. Agaricaceae and Amanitaceae family members are alike in several ways. They both usually have a stem, a cap, and gills that are free or unattached to the stem. Furthermore, members of both

families can have cups at their base and rings around their stems. However, a critical difference between the two families is spore color. While spores of Amanitaceae family members are generally white or yellowish white, those of Agaricaceae members are dark, reddish brown or black. What's most important in application is that most members of Amanitaceae are very poisonous, sometimes deadly, while many in Agaricaceae are choice edibles. One would not want to learn this distinction the hard way.

Noticing a mushroom's location on the ground or on wood, and within its surrounding plant or tree community also helps significantly when trying to identify it. The following examples illustrate this point. The locally common *Agaricus campestris*, also commonly known as the meadow mushroom, grows up from the ground, not from wood, in open grassy areas like lawns and meadows. It is also a cousin of the popular grocery store mushroom, *Agaricus bisporus*. Another species that shows up in local lawns is the poisonous, green-spored lepiota or parasol mushroom, *Chlorophyllum molybdites*.

Russula mariae, a very attractive red to purple capped mushroom also grows up from the ground. It is mycorrhizal with oaks and other hardwoods, so should be looked for in those tree communities. The striking orange-yellow *Laetiporus sulphureus*, also known as chicken mushroom or sulphur fungus, grows most often on oak, either on fallen dead logs or relatively high above the ground on living trees. Its close relative and look-alike, *Laetiporus cincinnatus*, also grows on dead or living oaks, but at the bases of the live trees. Thus, paying close attention to where and how a particular mushroom grows can prove useful in leading to its identification.

Especially when identifying mushrooms for culinary reasons, one is wise to be cautious. In addition to making detailed notes of all the aforementioned characteristics and habits, one should pay close attention to the species' growth stages. Some stages of one species may look similar to later stages of another species. For example, a newly emerging *Amanita bisporigera*—the most common of those white amanitas colloquially known as "destroying angels" because of their poisonous nature—can look very much like a small edible puffball. Cross-referencing the species to ensure that it is considered an edible is also recommended. Finally, even when determined as edible, only small amounts of any mushroom should be ingested the first few times. Mushrooms considered edible by most can give certain people undesirable reactions.

It's reassuring to realize that even though the way science organizes them will continue to change, these fascinating organisms will not. Reliably, they will emerge in the same areas, year after year. Thus, learning them and building a knowledge base of the varied and beautiful local species of mushrooms can be a rewarding and enriching passion.

Some recommended websites on fungi are listed in the section on Natural History Resources after Chapter 10.

CHAPTER FIVE

Wildlife Across the County

This chapter is about the animal species that are widespread and found in many habitats across the county. These animals have adapted well to places intensively altered by humans: cities, suburbs, and farms. Some are relatively easy to see. Others, though abundant, often escape our notice. More specialized animals, confined mostly to the places we call "natural areas;" e.g., the Metroparks, state parks and preserves, and wildlife refuges—are treated in later chapters.

Common Mammals of Lucas County

The most conspicuous wild mammals in the county, familiar to nearly everyone, are the big tawny Fox Squirrels. They may be found wherever there are trees, from densely-settled urban areas to the

A doe and fawn at Side Cut Metropark one fall morning. (Photo by Art Weber)

forested tracts of the oak openings. Fox Squirrels can become very tame and are quick learners. In my yard they forage for spilled seed beneath the bird feeders, and one individual clearly has learned to associate me with food—she watches me fill the feeders and follows me instead of running away when I go outdoors. She might take bread or a nut from my hand if I offered it, but for their own safety as well as ours, I try not to encourage wild animals to be too confiding in humans.

White-tailed Deer are a classic example of a wild species adapting to the human-managed landscape. In pioneer times deer numbers were controlled by native predators, primarily wolves and cougars. It is also likely that the large expanses of dense forest and swamp that existed here then were not ideal deer habitats. Deer are essentially "edge" animals, feeding primarily in meadows and woods edges. With the removal of large predators, the clearing of forests, and the planting of crops and backyard gardens, deer have flourished. Numbers are especially high in the Metroparks and suburbs such as Maumee and Ottawa Hills, where they are accustomed to humans and have not been hunted. Deer are now verging on being a pest species, consuming flower and vegetable plantings, causing a hazard to cars on the roadways, leaving piles of droppings in residential yards, and creating five-foot high "browse lines" by consuming native wildflowers and woody undergrowth in some of our woodlands. Recogniz-

A fox squirrel at Secor Metropark. (Photo by Art Weber)

ing these problems, the Metroparks Toledo has begun a limited program of deer management, and in November 2015, the citizens of Ottawa Hills voted to allow bow hunters to cull deer inside the village limits.

The local deer population explosion is a relatively recent phenomenon, having occurred in just the past 50 years. As recently as 1970, the only way to be sure of seeing deer was to go to Mallard Lake in Oak Openings Preserve Metropark, where a few deer were kept in an enclosure next to the parking lot. The deer population explosion has provoked intense public controversy in some communities and remains a difficult issue to resolve to everyone's satisfaction.

Other common, familiar mammals include the Eastern Chipmunk, Eastern Cottontail Rabbit, woodchuck, Red Squirrel, and in the marshes near Lake Erie, the muskrat. Less familiar but also common is the Southern Flying Squirrel. This small, acrobatic squirrel sleeps through the day inside a tree hollow and feeds at night, so it is rarely seen even though it is numerous, especially in neighborhoods where there are oaks and other nut-bearing trees.

But our most abundant mammals are small creatures that often escape notice because they live mostly under leaf litter and dense grass. These include shrews, moles, and three rodents, the Meadow Vole, White-footed Mouse and Deer Mouse.

A flying squirrel, the most often overlooked squirrel in Lucas county. (Photo by Art Weber)

The Short-tail Shrew is abundant and widespread, although relatively few people are aware of its presence. It is a voracious predator on insects, worms, and other small animals, and also feeds on fresh carcasses of larger animals. Eastern Moles are also common, especially in areas with soft or sandy soil, suitable for burrowing. Moles feed belowground on worms and grubs and are not often seen, but their presence is easily detected by the raised sod above their tunnels. Among the rodents, Meadow Voles are grass eaters, and can reach high abundances in fallow fields and along highway rights-of-way that are not close-mowed. They are a favorite prey for hawks and owls, but their populations are cyclic, being very high in some years and low in others. White-footed and Deer Mice occur almost everywhere, and most often attract attention when they enter our homes. They are surprisingly good climbers and may forage

A warren of baby rabbits. (Photo by Art Weber)

up into bushes and small trees.

Bats are common here and are highly beneficial because they consume huge quantities of insects. At least eight species are known to occur here regularly. The most familiar species is probably the Big Brown Bat, which is the bat most likely to occur in residential areas. A Big Brown Bat has invaded our house on three occasions, and each time it has been a challenge to safely trap the animal and release it outdoors. Bats in other areas of the country have been dying from white-nose syndrome, an introduced fungal disease. Cave-dwelling bats seem especially vulnerable. So far there is little evidence of this disease in bats from Lucas County, but wildlife personnel are watching for it, and it is a cause for concern.

Raccoons and opossums may be encountered almost anywhere, even in urban areas. They are active mostly at night, but occasionally forage during the day. Although their long canine teeth suggest they are carnivores (meat-eaters), they are actually omnivorous opportunists, eating fruits, nuts, and seeds as well as small animals. Opossums are the only North American marsupials—pouch-bearing mammals whose young are born at a very early stage of development. Young opossums, the size of kidney beans at birth, creep up their mother's belly into her pouch and finish developing there, feeding on milk from the mother's nipples.

Raccoons are capable tree-climbers, and often

A big brown bat. (Photo by Art Weber)

spend the day snoozing in tree hollows. They also may climb to reach ripe fruits; one June evening we discovered a group of eight raccoons feeding in a small cherry tree next to our deck. Raccoons are very adept at manipulating objects with their paws, digging in marshes for clams and turning rocks in streams to capture crayfish. Raccoons are apparently quarrelsome; it is not unusual to hear their raucous growls and barks as they confront one another in the night.

Probably our third most common medium-sized carnivorous mammal is the Striped Skunk. Skunks have powerful front claws and do a great deal of digging for insect grubs and other prey. They often make their presence known by their powerful odor, a very effective defense mechanism. The source of the odor is scent glands at the base of the tail. These glands can be squeezed by powerful muscles, sending a foul spray as much as ten feet. During a Thanksgiving visit, my daughter's family brought along their dog. Let out into the yard one night, he encountered a skunk and got sprayed in the face. A scrubbing down with a mixture of dish detergent, hydrogen peroxide and baking soda was fairly effective, but the dog's breath still smelled of skunk four days later when they departed for home. Road-killed skunks apparently spray when they are hit, leaving a lingering "perfume" in the air that may last for several days.

Top, a least weasel peers over a log. A pair of young raccoons, left. (Photos by Art Weber)

The red fox is a valuable predator on mice and other small rodents. (Photo by Art Weber)

The coyote has probably been in Lucas County for many years, but because it tends to avoid human contact its true abundance is hard to assess. Based on the number of recent sightings, its numbers may be increasing. Coyotes are generally disliked because of occasional depredations on small livestock, and where common they are known to reduce populations of wild competitors such as foxes. On balance they may be beneficial as controllers of small rodents and rabbits, but this is uncertain. What is certain is that the wily coyote will be with us for the foreseeable future. Both Red and Gray Foxes occur in Lucas County as well, although both appear to be declining with the increase of coyotes and continuing land clearance for houses and commercial sites.

One other carnivore deserves mention. It is not native, and, like many introduced species, it causes great harm to our native wildlife. The house cat is an efficient predator whose natural instinct is to hunt and kill small mammals and birds. Even well-fed pet cats, if allowed outdoors, will do this repeatedly. A recent study by biologists of the U.S. Fish & Wildlife Service and Smithsonian Institution estimated that cats kill as many as 3.7 billion birds and up to 20 bil-

A chickadee killed by housecat.
(Shutterstock photo)

along the Maumee River. Remarkably, in 2005 a young black bear made an appearance at the western edge of Lucas County. It probably wandered into our area from Michigan, where the bear population is expanding. Unfortunately, this particular bear was struck and killed by a vehicle. Even more remarkably, in 2014 one or more bobcats were seen in the oak openings area in the western part of the county. Like the bear, one bobcat also came to an unfortunate end under the wheels of a vehicle.

These deaths point to a serious threat to our wildlife—the likelihood of becoming a road-kill. The number of road-killed animals along our highways is astounding. The most frequent victims appear to be raccoons, opossums, and Fox Squirrels. It is not clear whether some aspect of their behavior makes them especially vulnerable, or whether this pattern simply reflects their abundance relative to other species.

It is surprising that despite the huge numbers road-killed every year, these mammals apparently continue to flourish. When collisions involve large mammals, the danger extends to humans and their vehicles. Deer, which often weigh over 100 pounds, can seriously damage a car and its occupants. Since deer have become so abundant, drivers must be constantly aware of the possibility that a deer will dash into the road in front of them. This danger is especially acute at night and in the fall, when deer are mating.

Tip: If a doe dashes across the road in front of you in the fall, wait a few extra seconds. A buck may be chasing her. This knowledge has saved me from at least one collision.

lion small mammals every year in the United States. There are about 84 million pet house cats in the U.S., and there are also unknown numbers—the low estimate is 30 million—of feral (wild) cats, animals that have either escaped from captivity or been dumped out on purpose by owners who no longer wanted them. Cats should be kept indoors to avoid unnecessary deaths to wildlife.

An interesting and reassuring trend in recent years has been the reappearance of several native mammals that were extirpated from northwest Ohio more than 100 years ago. In the past decade, beavers have reinvaded both the Lake Erie marshes and western Lucas County tributaries (e.g., Swan Creek in the Oak Openings).

Evidence of River Otters also has been noted several times recently in the Lake Erie marshes and

Common Birds of Lucas County

Lucas County is in a fortunate location for both birds and bird-watchers. The county is rich in birdlife in all seasons. The book *Birds of the Toledo Area* (see references) lists 357 species, and since that book was published in 2002 an additional eighteen species have been recorded here. Migrating birds following the Ohio and Mississippi River valleys are funneled northward into our area along the Wabash and Maumee Rivers, and migrants that hesitate to cross large bodies of water "pile up" along the Lake Erie shore in spring. Some cross eventually, but many others detour around the western end of Lake Erie, passing directly through Lucas County. Also, several species of waterfowl that winter along the Atlantic coast cross the Appalachians and stop to feed in the wetlands along the lake's southwest shore. Because so many songbirds, shorebirds and waterfowl pass through our area, it has been recognized as a globally significant migrant stopover site. Finally, the annual Toledo Christmas Bird Count (CBC), conducted on a single day in mid-December, holds the all-time Ohio CBC record of 110 species, set in 2013.

There simply isn't enough space to mention all the common birds of the county here. This section attempts to hit the high points, covering twenty birds that are widely distributed and may be encountered almost anywhere—birds the average person is most likely to see. For more, readers should see *Birds of*

An American Robin. (Photo by Art Weber)

the Toledo Area, which covers all the birds and directs you to some of the best places to see them.

Birds not usually seen at feeders

Any discussion of common birds must begin with the American Robin. Robins are probably the most abundant bird in North America, whose numbers may exceed the number of people in the United States—over 320 million. During the warmer months they are a familiar sight on our lawns, where they search for earthworms and other small prey. Over 60 years ago robins were regarded as harbingers of

spring, since they migrated south in November and we rarely saw them again until early March. But in recent years, as winters became milder, robins expanded their winter ranges northward. Now it is normal to see robins all year long in Lucas County. In winter they are especially attracted to fruiting trees and shrubs.

Birds of prey include the vultures, hawks, eagles, falcons, and owls. Twenty species of birds of prey occur regularly in Lucas County. The two birds of prey people are mostly likely to notice are the Turkey Vulture and the Red-tailed Hawk. Vultures are large soaring birds, mostly black, with naked red heads. They soar with wings tilted up, a good identification feature, noticeable even at a distance. Turkey Vultures are scavengers of dead animals and perform a valuable service by removing decaying carcasses from our roadways. In spring and fall, large flocks of migrating vultures often may be seen passing overhead.

Big Red-tailed Hawks often perch upright on poles, fences or trees along highways. Adults have orange tails visible in flight, but the easiest way to recognize all red-tails is by their white chests, visible when they are perched. Like all birds of prey, they feed on other animals, preferably mice, voles, rats, rabbits, and other small mammals. Although many Red-tailed Hawks pass over Lucas County in migration, others nest and remain here through the

A Red-tailed hawk at Blue Creek Metropark. (Photo by Art Weber)

Canada geese and goslings. (Photo by Art Weber)

winter. Hawks, eagles and falcons have remarkable vision. They can see a mouse in a grassy field, hundreds or even thousands of feet away.

One of our biggest avian success stories is the return of the Canada Goose. In the 1940s geese did not nest in Lucas County. Then state wildlife biologist Karl Bednarik established a goose breeding program in Magee Marsh at the eastern edge of the county. The program was very successful, and by the 1960s geese had established breeding populations across the Lake Erie marshes. The goose population continued to expand, and now geese nest on ponds and lakes across most of Ohio. But can success be carried too far? The advent of milder winters and the availability of waste corn in stubble fields have changed migratory patterns. Formerly geese

migrated out of our area for the winter, but now flocks of 100 or more may be seen feeding on lawns and fields throughout the year. Such high densities of geese can pollute feeding areas and ponds with droppings and may even create traffic hazards along nearby roads.

The other waterfowl species you are most likely to see is the mallard. The mallard is abundant throughout the year. For the most part, it nests in marshes and pond edges, but occasionally females will build nests in odd places. One year a mallard built a nest under a bush in our yard and stayed on her eggs even when I came within six feet with the lawn mower. Unfortunately (but not surprisingly), the eggs were destroyed long before their hatching time, probably taken in the night by a raccoon or other predator.

Mallards often join geese to feed in corn stubble fields during the colder months, and roost in large numbers on the Maumee River rapids when most of the river is frozen. Twenty species of ducks occur regularly in our area, most of them as migrants or winter visitors. More on waterfowl can be found in the chapter on Lake Erie and its marshes.

The European Starling is a chunky, short-tailed bird slightly smaller than a robin. It is most noticeable in fall and winter, when large flocks may be seen feeding in fields, perched on wires, or roosting in trees. In spring and early summer, starlings are

A mallard, top, at Howard Marsh Metropark and a European Starling, left. (Photos by Art Weber)

iridescent black with yellow beaks. But in late summer their beaks turn dark, and they molt into plumage speckled with white (thus the name "starling"). Originally brought to the U.S. from Europe in the 1891, Starlings are widely regarded as pests. They occasionally damage corn and orchard crops, and compete aggressively for holes with native woodpeckers, bluebirds, and other cavity-nesters.

In summer every wetland, no matter how small, may host one or more pairs of Red-winged Blackbirds. Male redwings even set up linear territories along ditches lining our interstate highways. They are easily recognized by their red and yellow shoulder patches, but female redwings look nothing like the males, and often mystify the casual observer. Females are heavily streaked with brown and are noticeably smaller than the males. Like the starling, redwings form large flocks in fall and winter. From October into April, aggregations of thousands of redwings may be encountered in the Lake Erie marshes, or feeding on the ground in corn stubble fields. Blackbirds and starlings sometimes flock together; in flight, blackbirds can be distinguished from starlings by their longer tails and undulating (bouncing) flight.

The Common Grackle is another abundant flock former. Like the redwing, grackles are members of the blackbird family. They are larger than robins, with sturdy beaks, pale yellow eyes, and black plumage glossed on the head with blue. Females are smaller and duller-looking than males, but all grackles can be identified by their yellow eyes and relatively long, wedge-shaped tails. Grackles are omnivorous,

Red-winged blackbird at Howard Marsh Metropark.
(Photo by Art Weber)

and will raid the nests of smaller birds, feeding on both eggs and nestlings. In fall, flocks often invade woodlands in the Oak Openings, sweeping through the forest, feeding on acorns as they go. On one September day, I encountered a grackle flock streaming across Girdham Road in Oak Openings Preserve. I estimated the number of birds crossing in a minute and watched until the last grackle was gone. My final estimate was 14,400 birds, and they had been crossing for a while before I arrived. Flocks of starlings, redwings, and grackles occasionally do visit feeders, making access difficult for smaller birds.

American Crows may be seen almost anywhere. They are aggressive and intelligent omnivores. On my street they seem to know when it's garbage day. Every Monday they sit in the trees lining the street, waiting for people to put their plastic garbage bags at the curb. Then the crows peck open the bags,

pulling out chicken bones, pizza crusts, and other food scraps, tossing foil, plastic wrap, corncobs, banana peels, and other inedibles into the street. Like the grackles, crows prey on the eggs and young of other birds. One year I watched a pair of crows methodically extract and eat the eggs from two Blue Jay nests on my property. Several years ago, crows suffered substantial losses due to West Nile virus (transmitted by mosquitoes), but their numbers seem to have stabilized.

Mourning Doves are identified by their chunky bodies, small heads, pointed tails, and habit of perching on overhead wires. Doves are especially abundant in farm country. Flocks may descend onto fields in fall and winter to feed on waste grain, but doves are also common in suburban yards, where their cooing calls are a frequent background noise in spring and summer. In winter, they will come to the ground beneath backyard feeders, foraging on seed spilled by other birds. The Mourning Dove makes one of the skimpiest nests of any bird, often just enough twigs placed in a low tree or vine tangle to barely support a couple of eggs. It is not surprising that dove nests often fail, but the bird compensates by having a very long nesting season, trying multiple times a year, if necessary, to bring off young. Like all doves and pigeons, Mourning Doves feed their nestlings a milk-like substance secreted by the lining of the crop, a sac at the base of the bird's esophagus.

A mourning dove at Oak Openings Preserve Metropark. (Photo by Christine Manzey)

A Cooper's hawk (far left) at Oak Openings Preserve Metropark. (Photo by Art Weber)

A hummingbird (top) at Secor Metropark. (Photo by Art Weber)

A Kestrel at Howard (left) at Marsh Metropark. (Photo by Art Weber)

Doves are fast flyers, exploding suddenly from cover when startled, their wings making a whistling sound.

Birds commonly seen at feeders

The last ten species are likely to be seen at bird feeders. Feeding birds has become a very popular activity. Most people feed birds during the colder months, but birds will visit feeders throughout the year if food is provided. Research studies suggest that most birds survive well in winter without supplemental feeding; but bird feeders certainly do birds no harm, provide us with a chance to observe interesting bird behavior, and bring much beauty to our yards during the long winter months. Even if you do not have a bird feeder, you can watch the feeders at the Windows on Wildlife at Pearson, Wildwood, Oak Openings, and other Metroparks.

The House Sparrow is a non-native bird, first introduced to the U.S. in 1851. It is not related to our native sparrows, belonging instead to a finch family (Ploceidae) of Europe and Africa. House Sparrows are dependent on humans to provide suitable habitat. They are generally absent from forests and other natural environments, but may be common in towns and cities, and in farmyards where waste grain is spilled on the ground. In close contact with humans they may lose all fear of people, hopping about underfoot where food is being served outdoors, and

Black-capped chickadee (top) and a white-breasted nuthatch (bottom). (Photos by Art Weber)

even straying indoors in garden centers and big box stores. House Sparrows commonly nest in holes or protected niches on man-made structures. They also nest in hollow snags and bird houses and compete with native hole-nesting songbirds for nest sites.

The most popular feeder bird is probably the Black-capped Chickadee. It is our smallest regular feeder visitor, weighing barely one-third of an ounce. Yet chickadees survive our coldest winter nights, conserving energy due to a remarkable ability to lower their body temperatures. They rapidly warm up at dawn, and then set out on an all-day quest for food to get them through the next cold night. One reason for chickadees' popularity is their tameness. Some feeder owners have "taught" chickadees to take food from the hand. Although I have resisted the temptation to do that, I am convinced that—like the squirrels—chickadees in our neighborhood associate me with being fed. They certainly have seen me refill the feeder. Often, when I go out into the yard, chickadees will fly in from the woods, investigate the feeder, and fly about just over my head, calling. Nuthatches in our yard exhibit the same behavior.

The White-breasted Nuthatch is common where there are sufficient large trees to provide feeding opportunities and holes for nesting. Nuthatches feed on a mixture of nuts and seeds, as well as invertebrates gleaned from the trunks and large branches of trees. While feeding they frequently move upside down, hitching down as well as up tree trunks.

Another common feeder visitor is the Tufted Titmouse. The titmouse has gradually expanded its range northward as winters have become less severe; the writings of nineteenth century naturalists suggest the bird was rare here 125 years ago. Titmice, chickadees and nuthatches form mixed-species flocks in fall and winter. They travel together and usually visit feeders together. They take turns at the feeder, but the larger species frequently displace the smaller ones from prime perches.

The Downy Woodpecker is the smallest local woodpecker, and a frequent participant in mixed feeding flocks led by chickadees and titmice. Like all woodpeckers, downies drill into trees to extract live

Tufted titmouse. (Photo by Art Weber)

prey, but they also come readily to suet and seed feeders. Male downies have a red spot on the back of their heads; otherwise males and females are virtually identical. An interesting observation is that on average, males feed on narrower twigs and stems than the slightly larger females, although there is plenty of overlap. One theory for this pattern is that the partitioning of feeding perches reduces competition for food between males and females occupying the same territory.

Blue Jays are among our most beautiful birds, but because they are so familiar we often take their beauty for granted. Like their relatives the crows, jays are highly intelligent. They are also noisy, and their alarm calls when a hawk is detected are a signal for other birds to take cover. Alternatively, groups of jays may "mob" a hawk or owl, flying as close as they dare while uttering a coarse grinding noise. The mobbing call often brings smaller birds in to investigate. Although we see jays in our yards all year long, the majority of our jays are migratory, spending the winter in the southeastern states along the U.S. Gulf coast. During the months of April, May, September and October, it is possible to see flocks of hundreds or even thousands of jays passing overhead on their migratory journeys. This phenomenon is especially striking in spring along the Lake Erie shore; at Cedar Point National Wildlife Refuge one early May morning, we estimated at least 3,300 jays passed overhead, moving west along the shoreline to avoid flying out over the open waters of the lake.

Northern Cardinals may be found anywhere there are trees and bushes to provide cover and nest sites. The male's bright red color probably accounts for the cardinal being the official bird of seven states, including Ohio. The buff-colored female is less striking, but shares the male's red beak, crest, wings, and tail. Immature cardinals have dark beaks for the first few months after hatching. Cardinals

Left: A female downy woodpecker. (Photo by Art Weber)

Facing page: A blue jay. (Photo by Art Weber)

are attracted to feeders providing sunflower seeds, which they easily open with their thick beaks. Individual cardinals are non-migratory, but cardinals have expanded their ranges northward gradually as the winter climate has moderated and bird feeding has become increasingly popular. The first naturalists visiting Lucas County in the 1800s did not mention the cardinal; it has become common here only in the past 100 years or so.

American Goldfinches, sometimes called "wild canaries," are among the latest-nesting birds in our area. They often do not nest before July and may bring young off well into September. In winter they are common visitors to bird feeders, especially those providing sunflower seeds. The lemon-yellow males, with their black wings and black caps, are familiar to many people. But the males only wear their bright yellow feathers from April to September. For the other six months, they look like the much duller females. I once hosted a visiting birder friend from Great Britain who was very eager to see American Goldfinches. Unfortunately, it was November, and he was very disappointed to discover that none of the goldfinches at my feeder were yellow.

Any discussion of feeder birds must include the House Finch. Originally, House Finches occurred only in western North America. But in the 1920s House Finches were discovered near New York City. Apparently, some had been transported eastward illegally as cage birds, and had either escaped or been

A male Cardinal at Secor Metropark. (Photo by Art Weber)

released on purpose. After a lag of about 30 years, the eastern House Finch population exploded. They first appeared in Lucas County in 1978 and are now a common visitor to bird feeders in all seasons.

In fact, at times flocks of House Finches can be so large as to monopolize a feeder. House Finches are sparrow-sized birds, heavily streaked with brown. Males usually have pink breasts and rumps, although there is a lot of color variation. House Finch numbers have fluctuated since their arrival here; they are vulnerable to a fungal disease that infects their eyes and is often fatal. The final feeder bird is the Dark-eyed Junco. It may visit elevated feeders, but prefers to feed on the ground beneath, eating seed spilled by other birds. The sparrow-sized junco is one of our most abundant and familiar winter birds,

An American Goldfinch. (Photo by Art Weber)

arriving in late October and staying well into April. Juncos are readily recognized by their white outer tail feathers, visible as the bird flies away. Males are coal-black, females gray – although many birds are intermediate in color and difficult to attribute to either sex. Males are slightly heavier and tend to winter farther north than the females. In my yard, I generally see a lot of female-plumaged birds in fall and spring, whereas the majority of birds in January and February appear to be males.

Amphibians and Reptiles
By Kent Bekker

Herpetologists rarely view Lucas County as a Mecca for finding amphibians and reptiles. Despite this, Lucas County has a long history of amphibian and reptile study, with both taxa receiving the early attentions of Charles Walker (*The Amphibians of Ohio, Part 1. Frogs and Toads,* 1946) and Roger Conant (*The Reptiles of Ohio,* 1951). Several species

A Dark-eyed Junco. (Photo by Art Weber)

are found across the county in suitable habitats. Within our more unique ecosystems, like the Oak Openings or the Lake Erie marshes, other species can be found to be very abundant and conspicuous, but those species are not distributed throughout the county.

Several amphibians can be found throughout the county. For most of these species, suitable habitat is virtually any location with an ephemeral water source for reproduction. Several frogs and toads fall into this category. In addition to the frogs and toads, Lucas County has one very widespread salamander, the Red-backed Salamander. The Red-backed Salamander is unique in our region for having a direct development life cycle. Unlike most other amphibians, which have a free swimming larval stage (often called a tadpole), amphibians with direct development pass through the larval portion of their life cy-

cle within the egg. This unique strategy reduces the Red-backed Salamander's dependence on water, only requiring a moist area under a log or rock to deposit and guard their eggs. The Red-backed Salamander is a member of the lungless salamander family (Plethodontidae). As the name implies, Red-backed Salamanders do not have lungs; they absorb all the oxygen they need through their skin, which requires a moist environment and slender body shape.

American Toads are one of the most common and abundant amphibians in Lucas County. The American Toad has an aquatic tadpole stage; however, the tadpole stage only needs water for a period of 50 to 60 days. Adult American Toads are less reliant on moisture than other amphibians and as a result can be found in habitats well removed from water. Their calls are often heard in the spring from

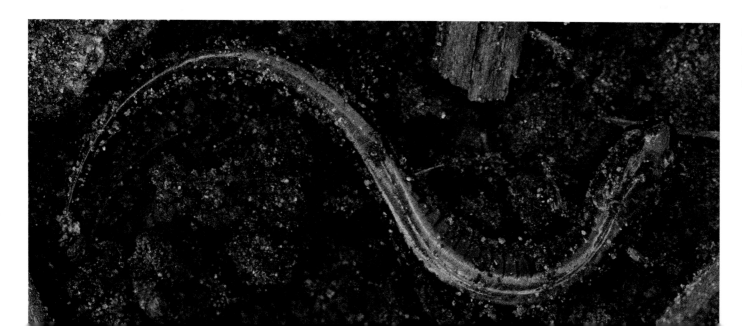

A Red-backed slamander. (Photo by Art Weber)

many shallow wetlands. The characteristic long loud trill is unmistakable.

Most permanent water bodies in the county contain Green Frogs and Bullfrogs. These species have a longer larval period than most other frogs or toads in the region. Green Frog larvae can overwinter, and Bullfrog larvae do overwinter. This long larval period prohibits their colonization of ephemeral wetlands that may dry out during this critical period of their development. These two large frogs are similar-looking, but the Green Frog has a raised ridge of skin along each side of the back that the Bullfrog lacks. The calls of both species are conspicuous in the mid-summer and are often confused with each another. The Bullfrog's "jug-o-rum" call is a low-pitched grumble, whereas the Green Frog's single

An American toad (above) and a wood frog tadpole (below). (Photos by Art Weber)

A bullfrog. (Photo by Art Weber)

note ("spung") sounds like plucking on a loose banjo string.

Several species of reptiles can be found throughout the county in suitable habitat. Two species of turtles and three snakes fall into this category. Painted Turtles are the species most often seen basking on logs during the summer months. Like most of our aquatic turtles, the Painted Turtle spends its entire winter on the bottom of wetlands. During this period a turtle's energy demands are so limited due to the cold and their ectothermic nature that sufficient oxygen can be absorbed through special tissue, generally the linings of the mouth and cloaca (ectothermic animals' body temperatures are regulated by the external environment).

Although the Snapping Turtle is less conspicuous

A snapping turtle at Howard Marsh Metropark. (Photo by Art Weber)

it is probably no less abundant than the Painted. Extremely catholic in its habitat preference, it can be found in ditches, ephemeral wetlands, and lakes. While stories and concern abound related to the Snapping Turtle's ability to consume game fish and ducks, it consumes more plant material than most people appreciate, and in general consumes less food for its size than any warm blooded (endothermic) mammal or bird.

Eastern Garter Snakes are one of Lucas County's

most commonly encountered snake species. They are found in many different habitats. They consume a large diversity of food items, ranging from earthworms to small mammals. Like most of the snakes in our region, the Eastern Garter Snake is viviparous; i.e., it does not lay eggs but gives birth to live young in mid-summer.

The Brown Snake or Dekay's Snake is one the smallest snakes in the region. It specializes in slugs as a food item. Being one of the smallest snakes, it produces one of the smallest offspring: young are born about three inches long. This species is commonly encountered in vacant urban lots where refuge and food are available.

The Northern Water Snake is dependent on aquatic habitats, but this habitat can vary as long as the primary food source of fish is available. Where fish are abundant, like Round Gobies in Lake Erie, the Northern Water Snake can achieve very high densities. Water snakes play an integral role in our local food web, cycling nutrients from aquatic environments to terrestrial, as they form a food source for some of our bird species.

It should be noted that although there were rattlesnakes in the region when the first Europeans arrived, there have been no records of venomous snakes in Lucas County for many decades.

An Eastern Garter snake (above). (Photo by Kent Bekker)

A Brown snake, or Dekay's snake, at Secor Metropark (right). (Photo by Art Weber)

Insects and other Arthropods

Arthropods are animals with jointed legs (that is what "arthropod" means) and hard exoskeletons encasing their bodies. Local examples include insects, spiders, ticks, mites, isopods, millipedes, centipedes, and crayfish. Insects have six legs; spiders, ticks and mites have eight. Other arthropods may have ten or more.

On a world-wide basis, insects are the most diverse group of animals, with close to one million species having been described. No one knows the true number of insect species; even well-explored places like Ohio may harbor small insect species that no one has studied or named. Insects are crucially important members of natural communities. Some are beneficial to humans. Bees pollinate a wide variety of flowering plants, including most of our fruits and vegetables. Flies, isopods and some beetles and mites aid in the decay of dead material. Lacewings and ladybug beetles help control plant-sucking aphids, and spiders, dragonflies and damselflies prey on a wide variety of insects, including biting flies and mosquitoes. Finally, butterflies enrich our lives aesthetically with their beautiful colors and ornate wing patterns.

But we also recognize that many insects are our competitors, and some are disease vectors. Billions of dollars are spent every year to prevent insects

A bee nectating on butterfly weed at Blue Creek Metropark. (Photo by Art Weber)

from consuming our fruits, vegetables and grains, and despite those expenditures crop losses to insects are in the many millions of dollars. Major agricultural pests include caterpillars of many species, aphids, beetles, and grasshoppers. Mosquitoes are vectors of a number of serious diseases, including malaria, yellow fever, encephalitis, and recently, West Nile and Zika viruses. Most people are probably unaware that malaria and yellow fever were fairly common in Lucas County when the first European settlers arrived and persisted well into the 1800s. Fortunately, these diseases have been eradicated in our area, and for the most part, mosquitoes now are more of a nuisance than a serious disease threat. Among the non-insect arthropods, ticks are vectors of potentially serious diseases, including spotted fever and Lyme disease.

Here we will mention some arthropod groups that have a major impact on our landscape; clearly, an exhaustive treatment of our local arthropods is far beyond the scope of this book. Most are small—some even microscopic—and even our largest ones rarely exceed a couple of inches in length and weigh far less than an ounce—so their impact is felt through their sheer numbers, which can be very large indeed.

When we think of bees, generally two thoughts come to mind. One, they can sting, and two, they pollinate flowers. Actually, some bees cannot sting,

A praying mantis on goldenrod flowers at Secor Metropark. (Photo by Art Weber)

and not all of them are important pollinators. Honeybees, introduced deliberately from Europe in the seventeenth century, are important pollinators of many of our fruits and vegetables, which is not surprising, since many of our fruits and vegetables are of Eurasian origin as well. But many native bees (e.g., mason bees and bumblebees) are also efficient pollinators, so fortunately we are not entirely reliant on honeybees.

Close relatives of bees, the wasps and hornets, perform a variety of functions. Many are omnivores, feeding on spiders, other insects and their larvae, but also eating ripe fruit and scavenging dead materials. The most familiar of these is the Yellow Jacket. Yellow Jackets and related species may form colonies that nest in the ground, or in closed higher spaces—during two recent summers we have had a nest inside the walls of our house.

The Bald-faced Hornet builds the familiar soccer ball-sized gray nests, noticeable hanging in trees after the leaves fall. Usually by October the nests are empty, and all the hornets have died except one or more queens. The queens have been fertilized by male hornets ("drones"). Each queen overwinters in a sheltered spot—often under a log—and emerges in spring to begin building a new nest. She lays eggs in the chambers, and soon her offspring emerge to help. Her female offspring can produce additional workers, so the colony grows rapidly to 400 or more individuals. Thus, the nest grows through the sum-

A bald-faced hornet emerges from its nest. (Photo by Art Weber)

mer. Before the frost, the old queen and all drones and workers die, but before they do one or more new queens are produced to repeat the cycle.

Many years ago, a graduate student and I were seining fish in Tenmile Creek. We swept the net under the bank beneath some low-hanging branches—often a good hangout for a large fish—and as we pulled up the seine my head bumped a hornet nest. Immediately I was stung at least four times on the back of the neck. We threw down the net and staggered away. The pain was intense, but fortunately the hornets did not continue to attack once we were twenty feet away. Active Bald-faced Hornet nests are fiercely defended and should be given a wide berth.

Ants are noticed mainly when they invade our homes, but in nature they are among the most important arthropods. They have a profound influence on the landscape because of their huge numbers. Their activities aerate and excavate the soil, and a colony will consume immense quantities of food each year—the food eaten varying widely depending on the species. Even more abundant in the soil are tiny arthropods, the mites and springtails. Mites are eight-legged animals closely related to spiders; springtails are tiny flightless six-legged animals that can spring many times their height into the air by flexing a forked tail-like appendage that folds under the body when they are at rest. Mites may be predators, plant eaters, or litter decomposers, depending on the species. Most springtails are decomposers, feeding on dead plant material.

We notice butterflies and appreciate their beauty. But their close relatives, the moths, are much more abundant and diverse. We tend to pay less attention to them because they are active mainly at night, and most are small and drab-brown. But most of the caterpillars that damage crops and garden plantings are the larvae of moths, so one could argue that moths are far more important than butterflies. Just the same, iconic butterflies like the Monarch have significance far beyond their economic value, because they enrich our lives and help to stimulate interest in the preservation of nature.

The most diverse insects, by far, are the beetles. Beetles comprise a significant percentage of all animal species that have ever been described. When a member of the clergy asked eminent British biologist J.B.S. Haldane what he learned about the Deity from a study of living things, he is supposed to have responded, "The Lord has an inordinate fondness for beetles." Some beetles are brightly colored, some are serious crop and garden pests, and a few are large and have spectacular horns or other growths on their shells. For many gardeners, the best-known beetle is an introduced pest, the Japanese Beetle, which consumes a wide variety of leaves and flowers of species in the rose family. The familiar firefly is actually a soft-shelled beetle. Like butterflies, beetles have a complex life cycle involving four stages, egg, larva, pupa, and adult. Many beetle larvae live in the soil, consuming the roots of plants.

Dragonflies and damselflies are widespread, although generally absent from forest interiors. They are voracious predators on other insects, which they typically capture on the wing. Close to 100 species

A cicada killer (above). A cicada killer drags a paralyzed cicada to its nest (right). (Photo by Art Weber)

have been recorded in Lucas County. The most easily-observed species include Common Blue Darner, Black Saddlebags, Widow Skimmer, and Common Whitetail. The latter two species often search for insect prey in our flower gardens. More on these predators may be found in Chapters 6 and 7.

Midges, flies and mosquitoes are in the Order Diptera. The name refers to the fact that these insects have only two wings rather than four. Most larvae of dipterans are either aquatic or live in soft decaying flesh or fruits. Midges and mosquitoes are in the former category; adult midges may emerge by the billions from lakes and marshes and form dense mating swarms. Mosquito larvae, on the other hand, require still water, so they favor stagnant floodplain pools and ditches, as well as habitats provided by humans, such as bird baths, gutters, discarded tires, etc. Thus, it is very important for property owners to dump out any standing water at least once a week to prevent the emergence of mosquitoes from outdoor containers.

Everyone who lives where there are trees is familiar with the loud buzz of cicadas. Most of the cicadas in Lucas County are of the annual variety; that is, they live only one year. In July the adults emerge from underground, mate, and lay eggs in the twigs of deciduous trees. The eggs hatch and the young (called nymphs) drop to the ground and burrow underground along tree roots. Once they are deep enough to avoid winter frost, they "plug in" to the vascular system of the host tree and feed on its sap. The next July they emerge, crawl up the tree trunk, split their skins and emerge as winged adults to repeat the cycle. They seem to do no lasting damage to the trees.

Grasshoppers, katydids, and crickets are common here as well. Grasshoppers are found mostly in fields and meadows, and they are also numerous on sand barrens in the Oak Openings. Bright green katydids favor deciduous trees and are frequently encountered in shaded suburban yards in late summer and early fall. After sunset, their strumming triplet calls replace the daytime buzz of the cicadas. Crickets live on the ground virtually everywhere there is vegetation. Their chirps provide a background to the evening chorus of katydids. Crickets chirp faster when it is warm; in fact, you can estimate the temperature from the frequency of their chirps using the following formula:

chirps in 14 seconds + 40 =
temperature in degrees F.

No treatment of arthropods would be complete without a brief mention of spiders, ticks and chiggers. Little love is lost on these animals, but it must be said that spiders are extremely beneficial. They consume huge numbers of mosquitos, flies, and moths, whose caterpillars compete with us for food. As noted earlier, ticks can transmit diseases, so one should do a complete body check for ticks after being outdoors in grass, shrubbery, or other vegetation. The idea is to spot the tick before it has a chance to dig in. Ticks that have done so can be carefully removed with tweezers. Chiggers are so tiny as to be virtually invisible; they are related to ticks and live in a lot of the same places. They tend to bite warm areas of the body where clothing is tight, e.g. under socks, underwear elastic, bra lines, etc. Chiggers bite and then drop off, but a few hours later a red welt develops at the site, which can itch for up to a week. Treating clothes with repellent before going out helps to prevent chigger bites.

A wolf spider in Secor Metropark. (Photo by Art Weber)

CHAPTER SIX

The Oak Openings

As the last glacier retreated from our region, it temporarily blocked the outlet of Lake Erie. Waters of that ancient lake backed up, forming a shoreline in what is now the western portion of Lucas County. When the outlet finally opened, the lake drained eastward (over Niagara Falls) and eventually assumed its present-day level, leaving behind inland sand deposits, the remnants of beaches and sand bars marking the ancient shoreline. Those sand deposits underlie the region now known as the Oak Openings. Under the sand is a dense layer of clay and glacial till that is nearly impenetrable to water. The combination of nutrient-poor sandy soil and a high water table creates unusual conditions that support a diverse and unique array of plants and animals, and make the Oak Openings a region of global biological significance.

Lupines along Wilkins Road at Oak Openings Preserve Metropark. (Photo by Art Weber)

The Oak Openings: A Marvel of Biological Diversity

By Robert Jacksy, Jr.

Almost 200 species of Ohio's endangered, threatened, or potentially threatened plants have been identified in the Oak Openings. The original Oak Openings consisted of about 80,000 acres of mostly prairie and oak savanna habitats extending through Ohio's Lucas, Fulton and Henry counties and into three counties in southeast Michigan. While suburban sprawl and commercial development have consumed most of this land, a few far-sighted public agencies and conservation organizations have ownership of critical habitats. Metroparks Toledo manages about 4,700 acres, the Ohio Division of Natural Areas and Preserves holds 393 acres, the Ohio Division of Forestry has 3,068 acres, and The Nature Conservancy owns about 600 acres. Many private land owners have much smaller plots that they maintain as prairie or savanna.

Perhaps the most unique habitat in the Oak Openings is the oak savanna. Ohio savannas historically had two to twenty trees per acre. White oak and black oak were the most common trees, with understories dominated by grasses and sedges. Before Euro-American settlement, native peoples used fire as a land management tool. Fire kills many thin-barked trees such as maples, black cherry, American beech, and small shrubs, but often spares mature oak trees, which produced acorns for consumption by the natives. Fire also encouraged the growth of prairie grasses that the Indians would harvest to eat. These acorns and grasses also fed animals the Indians hunted: wild turkey, deer, elk, bison, and other game. The displacement of native cultures from the 1600s through 1800s spelled the end of the use of fire until the latter part of the twentieth century, when land managers rediscovered the benefits of its use.

The four previously-mentioned agencies have been using prescribed burns to reinvigorate prairie and savanna habitats. The results of these intentional, controlled fires have been nothing short of

Controlled burn at Blue Creek Metropark. (Photo by Art Weber)

Recently burned oak savanna at Oak Openings Preserve Metropark.
(Photo by Elliot Tramer)

astounding. Native plants such as wild lupine, fern-leaf false foxglove, junegrass, and many, many others have made a comeback from a very marginal existence. Some seeds of grassland species can persist for decades, in some cases even over a century, in the soil. Ecologists call this seed supply a seed bank. These seeds lay dormant if sunlight is blocked by thick leaf litter or an overly dense canopy. But if a disturbance such as fire clears away these growth inhibitors, the suppressed seeds can be free to germinate.

Oak Openings Preserve Metropark contains plant species that have not been found naturally occurring anywhere else in Ohio. Gay-wings, an attractive member of the milkwort family, is found at three sites in the Preserve. Sand serviceberry was recently discovered by keen-eyed botanist Tim Walters at a place where hundreds of naturalists have walked for decades, not noticing it as a rare species of serviceberry.

Two other unusual plants are porcupine grass and the spatulate-leaved sundew. The seeds of por-

Savanna sunset at Blue Creek Metropark.
(Photo by Art Weber)

cupine grass have a needle-sharp tip and its long awn is twisted, like a corkscrew. When dry, the awn shortens, and when moist it elongates. This change of lengths screws the shed seed into the ground. The sundew, which grows on wet sandy margins, is a carnivorous plant. It augments its nutritional needs by luring tiny insects to its nectar droplet-secreting leaflets. The insects are captured by adhesive in the sweet fluid and digested externally by the plant's secreted enzymes.

Awareness of the unique natural history of the Oak Openings region was catalyzed in 1928 when Professor Edwin L. Moseley's monograph, *Flora of the Oak Openings*, was published in *Proceedings of the Ohio Academy of Science*. Since his groundbreaking work, many other naturalists and scientists have added to the body of knowledge of this remarkable landscape. With this knowledge and awareness comes a great responsibility for wise stewardship of the remaining preserves. We now know that the Oak Openings depends on restorative fires to open the understories of the savannas and clear the prairies of invading shrubs. A measure of our generation's concern for Lucas County's natural history will be how well we managed the Oak Openings Region for its unique native biodiversity. We truly have been given an opportunity, a second chance, to get it right.

Rare Plants of the Oak Openings
By Dr. Tim Walters

Lucas County, due to the unusual soil and moisture conditions found in the Oak Openings, has always had more rare species and globally rare communities than anywhere else in Ohio. The county has led the state in rare plant species ever since the first rare plant list was created in 1980. A third of all of the rare vascular plants in the state are found in the Oak Openings region, a staggering proportion.

In his 1928 book *The Flora of the Oak Openings*, Edwin L. Moseley introduced the area to the botanical community. He listed 715 species he had found in this region and told of the uniqueness of the inland sand dunes and wet meadows. Presently approximately 1,260 vascular plant species have been found in the Oak Openings. 165 species of plants from the most current (2014-2015) Ohio rare species list have been recorded in the Oak Openings, although 24 of them are currently extirpated (locally extinct). Several of the extirpated species have not been seen in the region since Moseley first recorded them. Almost half of the 24 are from open wetlands that are no longer prevalent in this area. The 141 persisting Oak Openings species are listed as either potentially threatened, threatened or endangered in the State, the highest collection of rare species anywhere.

Approximately 45 percent of the rare plants of the Oak Openings Region only flourish in dry open sandy areas. In Oak Openings Preserve Metropark these areas are home to the low serviceberry (first

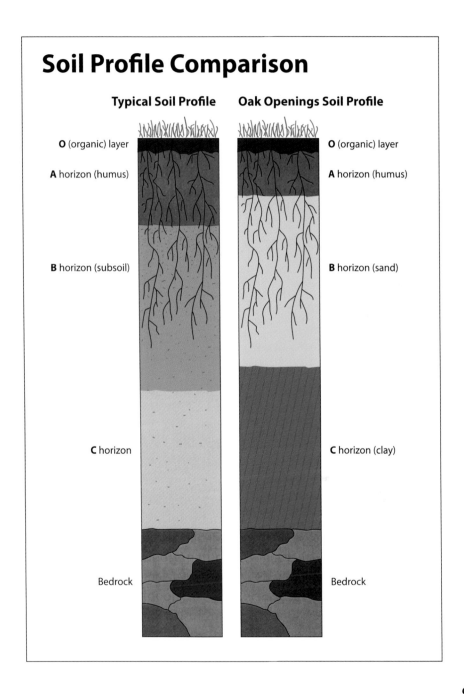

Soil Profile Comparison

Typical Soil Profile

O (organic) layer

A horizon (humus)

B horizon (subsoil)

C horizon

Bedrock

Oak Openings Soil Profile

O (organic) layer

A horizon (humus)

B horizon (sand)

C horizon (clay)

Bedrock

found in the state in 2014) and forked triple-awned grass (first discovered in 2006). More frequently encountered rarities include dwarf dandelion, purple triple-awned grass, wild blue lupine, hoary puccoon, sweet-fern, and dotted horsemint. Many of these along with eastern blue-eyed grass and the Lucas County-only Cleland's evening-primrose are found along trails of The Nature Conservancy's Kitty Todd Preserve.

An often overlooked, modest group of species comprise the Cistaceae or the rockrose family. All of the members of this family are on the Ohio rare plant list and all but one occur in the Oak Openings. Included are the frostweeds and pinweeds, all adapted to open barrens. Recently, a closer look at the blackberries or bristleberries has shown that there may be at least three undocumented rare species on these sandy barrens. Other species, like the showy goldenrod, scaly blazing-star and Greene's rush prefer more densely-vegetated prairie communities within the Oak Openings.

The wet meadow/prairie habitat contains 43 percent of the state-listed species found in the Oak Openings. Because these communities are so dependent on the level of the water table, even slight changes could cause the loss of much of the flora. The best remaining example of this habitat is Ir-

Left: Lupine and pucoon at Campbell Prarie in Oak Openings Preserve Metropark. (Photo by Art Weber)

Facing page: Dotted horsemint (left) and blazing star (right). (Photos by Art Weber)

win Prairie State Nature Preserve. A few of the wet prairie species noted by Moseley can no longer be found. But although these species are apparently gone, they may not be gone forever. In 2015, a long-lost species, the northern manna-grass was found along the boardwalk at Irwin Prairie. Management activities may bring others back. Other rare species that can be seen at Irwin Prairie include grass-leaved arrowhead, little yellow sedge, slender willow, wire-grass, and Kalm's St. John's-wort.

Wet depressions and wet meadows at Wildwood Preserve Metropark also hold rare treasures such as Long's sedge, Canadian St. John's-wort, lance-leaved violet, and meadow beauty. Many of our most beautiful wildflowers like fringed gentians, grass-pink orchid, and orange-fringed orchid are found in these communities. Unfortunately, several species have been lost from this community, including showy (gone in the 1950s) and white lady-slipper orchids (1970), the white fringed orchid (1924) and false asphodel (1926). But like the northern manna-grass, these species may reappear if appropriate conditions can be reinstated.

An unusual community included in the wet prairie category is the palustrine sand plain. This micro-community is a seasonally-saturated, mineral sand, water table driven community. It can be described as an area too wet for most perennial upland species and too dry for most perennial wetland species. These areas are often human-created (e.g., drying pond edges, borrow pits and tire ruts) where the dry sand has been excavated to the level of ground water interaction.

Originally, this community would have been dependent on large animal trails and wallows. Species of this specialized community are the northern appressed club-moss, two dwarf bulrushes, spatulate-leaved sundew, narrow-headed panic grass, and beak-rush. The rarest of these, Drummond's dwarf bulrush, had not been seen for almost twenty years before reappearing in 2013.

The final twelve percent of rare species are found in ponds or in forested areas (including planted pine forests). Dry forest rarities include cow-wheat, spotted coral-root (an orchid), fringed milkwort, and

Facing page: Sedge meadow at Irwin Prarie State Nature Preserve, covered in frost. (Photo by Art Weber)

Right: Spatule-leaved sundew at Kitty Todd Preserve. (Photo by Art Weber)

round-leaved dogwood. Moister forests may contain the long-bracted green orchid, least grape fern, and purple fringed orchid.

The planted pine stands formerly supported common oak fern, shinleaf, and one-flowered wintergreen. All these species are presently extirpated from the region. The latter two species were the only populations found in Ohio. There has always been a question of whether to protect a rare species that is dependent on a planted pine community for the conditions for survival. Presently many of the pine communities are declining, and management policy has favored thinning and removal of many of the stands.

Finally, marsh cinquefoil and grass-leaved pondweed are found in a few human-created ponds or deeper water areas of marshes. These ponds imitate deeper pools once found naturally in the Oak Openings wet prairies.

These rare species illustrate the importance of the dry prairie and wet prairie communities for the preservation of the high diversity of plants that we

Left: Dogwoods at Mallard Lake at Oak Openings Preserve Metropark. (Photo by Art Weber)

Facing page: Results of pine plantation thinning along Wilkins Road in Oak Openings Preserve Metropark. (Photo by Art Weber)

enjoy in the Oak Openings. Moseley (1928) wrote that he felt there were more species in the Oak Openings than all the remainder of the state of Ohio:

> When we consider that the total area of the Openings is not one-third as great as that of an average Ohio county, it seems rather remarkable that more than half of all the plants ... to be found in the state live in this small area.

It is up to us to keep this statement true.

Orchids of the Oak Openings
By Eric Durbin

Orchids are one of the world's most diverse families of flowering plants. More than 26,000 species have been described, many of them in the tropics. In popular culture, orchids are depicted as huge, exotic flowers, redolent with cloying fragrance, festooning mossy tree limbs in a shadowy jungle. It comes as a surprise then to many people to learn that wild orchids are a part of the native flora of the Oak Openings.

My recent surveys reveal that 26 orchid species have been reliably reported from the Oak Openings. Unlike the popular version, Oak Openings orchids are terrestrial, firmly rooted in the soil. A few species (yellow fringed-orchid, large yellow lady's-slipper) do produce big showy blossoms like those in a florist's corsage, but the majority has small, even inconspicuous, flowers that are white (downy rat-

tlesnake plantain, ladies'-tresses) or green (Loesel's twayblade, club-spur, and tubercled orchids). Only one (prairie ladies'-tresses) has a truly conspicuous scent, and it is pleasant and fresh.

The wet meadows of the Oak Openings once supported an abundance of orchids. Early accounts describe how the spectacular showy ladies'-slipper and exquisite pink calopogon were harvested for the flower trade and hauled away by the wagon load. Subsequent drainage schemes, intense droughts, and modern land development further ravaged orchid populations. Unfortunately, most orchids have very exacting requirements and are difficult to propagate.

Most of our species are now very scarce indeed. At this writing, eight species are listed as rare (endangered, threatened or potentially threatened) by the State of Ohio. Three species have not been seen in many years and are presumed extirpated, meaning totally wiped out in the area.

Curiously, three other orchids—helleborine (a non-native that occasionally shows up in flower beds and lawns), autumn coral-root and downy rattlesnake plantain—may be increasing in the Oak Openings. None were reported before 1975, but all are now well established.

The orchids a visitor is most likely to encounter are nodding ladies'-tresses in ditches and wet meadows, yellow ladies'-tresses in open oak woodlands, and lily-leaved twayblade in wet woods. They are widespread in the Oak Openings and persisting in relatively secure numbers.

Above: Yellow Ladies Slipper at Oak Openings Preserve Metropark. (Photo by Art Weber)

Right: Ladies Tresses at the Girdham Road sand dunes in Oak Opening Preserve Metropark. (Photo by Art Weber)

Oak Openings Ferns

Lucas County has a moderately rich fern flora, well-represented in natural areas in the Oak Openings, which is the best place to see most of our species. In oak savannas managed by frequent burning, bracken fern covers the ground and may be the single most abundant herbaceous plant. Its roughly triangular fronds may exceed three feet in height. Bracken is distributed almost world-wide, and is considered a pest in some countries because it invades pastures and is toxic to livestock.

Four other ferns are common in damp woodland locations and may be readily seen near the Buehner Center in Oak Openings Preserve Metropark. These are cinnamon, interrupted, royal, and sensitive ferns. Cinnamon and interrupted ferns are closely related and resemble one another. But cinnamon fern bears its spores on bare fuzzy stalks that are separate from the fronds, whereas the spore cases of interrupted fern grow off the midrib of the fronds, "interrupting" the leaflets—thus giving the fern its name.

Royal fern grows in wet shady spots; its fronds are the least fern-like of our common local species, and its sporophiles (spore-bearing stalks) persist long after the fronds have died back. The same is true of the wavy-leaved sensitive fern, which also prefers damp sites (though often not as waterlogged

Maidenhair fern at Oak Openings Preserve. (Photo by Art Weber)

Facing page: Royal fern at Oak Openings Preserve. (Photo by Art Weber)

as sites occupied by royal fern).

Another common species in the Oak Openings is marsh fern, a small, bright green fern that grows along sunny ditches. Another species, lady fern, bears comma-shaped spore cases on the undersides of its dissected leaflets. It may be found in drier woodlands of the Oak Openings region. Four uncommon species deserve brief mention: Christmas fern is readily recognizable by its evergreen foliage and Christmas stocking-shaped leaflets. Look for it on slopes, e.g., along ravines at Wildwood Preserve Metropark. Ebony spleenwort is another evergreen species with shiny black stems.

Rattlesnake fern is a small species of dense thickets, whose sporophile resembles the tail of a rattlesnake. Finally, the delicate maidenhair fern, with its circular arrangement of leaflets, may be seen in several locations along the trails at Wildwood Preserve.

Oak Openings Birds

The best time for bird watching in the Oak Openings region is probably late spring and early summer, because a remarkable variety of birds nest there. A June morning spent birding in the Openings can easily produce a list of over 50 species. The region is remarkable for the occurrence of nesting birds not typically found elsewhere in northwest Ohio. For example, range maps in bird field guides suggest that Summer Tanagers and Blue Grosbeaks should not be nesting so far north, but they are here. Similarly, northern species such as Golden-crowned Kinglet, Saw-whet Owl, Pine Siskin, and Red-breasted Nuthatch nest occasionally in the Openings, south of their normal summer ranges. Finally, for at least the past 85 years, the sand barrens of the Oak Openings have supported thriving colonies of Lark Sparrows, prairie birds whose nearest populations nest hundreds of miles further west.

Forested tracts in the Oak Openings provide the best habitat in northwest Ohio for raptors such as Red-shouldered and Broad-winged Hawks and Barred Owls. Pileated Woodpeckers, apparently extirpated from Lucas County before 1900, were rediscovered at Wildwood Preserve Metropark in the 1970s, and have nested in Oak Openings Preserve and Secor Metropark since the early 2000s. Neotropical migrant songbirds such as Acadian Flycatchers, Wood Thrushes, Veeries, Hooded Warblers, Ovenbirds, Rose-breasted Grosbeaks, and Scarlet Tanagers are regular summer residents in the Oak Openings, but scarce breeders elsewhere in the county.

Oak savanna habitats are the domain of the Red-headed Woodpecker, a bird largely absent from

Lark sparrow at the Girdham Road sand dunes at Oak Openings Preserve Metropark. (Photo by Art Weber)

Facing Page: A red-shouldered hawk. (Photo by Art Weber)

the rest of the county in summer. Summer Tanagers are especially attracted to the savanna's open oak groves, especially sites where oak parcels lie close to pine plantings.

The oak groves seem to be the best habitat for Whippoorwills, whose repetitious calls may be heard at dusk from May into late summer. Girdham Road in Oak Openings Preserve is an excellent place to listen for them.

Shrubby habitats of the Openings are also vitally important for birds scarce elsewhere in the county,

Barred owl (left) at Secor Metropark and pileated woodpecker (above). (Photo by Art Weber)

A female Rose-breasted Grosbeak (top) and a Willow
Flycatcher (above), at Oak Openings Preserve. (Photos by Art Weber)
A Red headed Woodpecker (right).

including Yellow-breasted Chat, Eastern Towhee, Brown Thrasher, Blue-winged Warbler, and White-eyed Vireo.

Eastern Bluebirds are a conspicuous Oak Openings success story. Sixty years ago they were scarce, but the installation of nest boxes in open areas throughout Oak Openings Preserve has brought them back. They are now numerous in both savannas and open fields where nest boxes are present, and have spread from the Metroparks into other suitable habitats across much of the rural landscape of western Lucas County.

Finally, the planted conifer groves in Oak Open-

ings Preserve and Maumee State Forest, though not native to the county, are important bird habitats, providing the county's only nesting opportunities for Red-breasted Nuthatches, Pine Warblers, Blue-headed Vireos, and rarely, Golden-crowned Kinglets.

In mid-September, a sizeable fraction of Canada's southbound Broad-winged Hawks is funneled around the western end of Lake Erie and passes directly over the Oak Openings. On a good weather morning in mid-September, it is possible to see hundreds or even thousands of these hawks lift out of the woodlots, spiral upward on rising air currents, and depart southwestward on their way to the American tropics—a truly unique avian spectacle.

No treatment of Oak Openings birds would be complete without mentioning Wild Turkeys and Indigo Buntings. Turkeys were part of the original fauna of the region, and were an important food source for native Americans and early European settlers. But turkeys were extirpated from the county by the late 1800s. In the 1990s the Ohio Division of Wildlife began to reintroduce turkeys to many areas of Ohio, including the Oak Openings. The effort has been wildly successful; a few winters ago during a heavy snow, we counted 37 turkeys in our back yard.

Indigo Buntings may be one of the most abundant nesting birds in the Oak Openings region. My point counts in Oak Openings Preserve (eighteen

White-eyed Vireo at Oak Openings Preserve Metropark. (Photo by Art Weber)

stops) frequently record at least 30 singing males. Yet these beautiful, small indigo-blue birds are not well known to non-birders. They typically return from their tropical winter areas in early May, and stay into September. Look for the bright blue males on exposed tree branches or wires as you drive through the metropark.

Right: An Indigo bunting.
(Photo by Art Weber)

Below: Wild turkeys are increasing in number and spreading. (Photo by Art Weber)

The Badger: A Special Oak Openings Mammal

Badgers are large burrowing carnivores, in Lucas County confined primarily to the Oak Openings where the sandy soil provides ideal conditions for digging. They feed mostly on small mammals, but will also kill and eat Woodchucks, which they dig out of their burrows using their powerful front claws. They spend the day underground, and are active mostly at night or at dawn when few people are out, so they are rarely observed.

In my 50 years of field work in Lucas County, I have seen only one live Badger. On a bright late May afternoon, I was standing at the edge of the Lark Sparrow field on Girdham Road. About twenty feet to my right was a burrow opening, which I assumed belonged to a Woodchuck. To encourage a Lark Sparrow to fly into view, I tried a birding trick—a series high-pitched squeaks. The squeak sometimes attracts small birds, apparently curious to find the source of the sound. As I squeaked, I became aware of a movement off to my right. Turning slowly, I found myself face to face with a Badger. His head and upper body were out of the burrow. Both motionless, we stared at each other. I felt prickles at the back of my neck.

After what seemed like several minutes but probably was only ten or fifteen seconds, the badger backed down into his hole. A bit shaky, I walked to my car and drove home. My wife had just arrived from school. "Wanna see a badger?" I yelled. "Sure!" She grabbed her camera and we jumped in the car and drove the two miles from our house to the park. We stood near the burrow. I squeaked. No response. We cautiously walked to the burrow and peered in. "Looks empty," my wife ventured. You could see down about two feet, then the tunnel made a sharp turn and headed in the direction of California. No badger in sight. Typical.

Oak Openings Rare Butterflies

By Jan Dixon

The Oak Openings supports eight special butterflies, scarce species that are absent from other parts of the county. The Frosted Elfin is an Ohio Endangered Species that lays only one brood of eggs per year and lives in oak savannas and forest margins. It emerges in early spring, about mid-April. The host plant for the Frosted Elfin is wild lupine.

The end of May is the time to look for the Dusted Skipper, an Ohio Species of Concern, also having only one brood per year. The larval host plants for the Dusted Skipper are grasses, including both little and big bluestem, which grow in dry habitats of barrens and oak savannas and fields.

The Karner Blue Butterfly, a Federal and Ohio Endangered Species, also emerges about the end of May. A second brood can be seen in July. The host plant for the Karner Blue is wild lupine, which is found in openings of oak savanna and barrens. Ants are a very important part of the Karner Blue's life cycle. Its larva is protected by ants which feed on a larval secretion called "honeydew." This butterfly has been bred in captivity at the Toledo Zoo, and released into several sites in the Oak Openings, where it is carefully monitored each year and its habitat studied and protected.

May also brings the Silver-bordered Fritillary, an

Karner blue butterflies. A male (top) and a female (bottom) at Oak Openings Preserve Metropark. (Photos by Art Weber)

Ohio Threatened Species, which has three broods per year, and flies from May into September. This species prefers wet meadows and moist prairies. Its larval host plants are violets. Due to its special status it is also carefully monitored.

The Persius Duskywing is an Ohio Endangered Species that has not been identified for many years in the Oak Openings. It is single brooded, flying in May and June in oak savannas and adjacent utility easements. The larval host plants are wild indigo and wild lupine. Due to the difficulty of identification—by dissection only—its current status in the Oak Openings is unknown.

Three more butterflies are rare and special in the Oak Openings. The Edwards' Hairstreak can be seen in July on prairie hills, ridges, forest margins, and oak barrens. It has only one generation per year and the local host plants are black and white oaks. The larva is tended by ants, like the larva of the Karner Blue Butterfly. Therefore, where you encounter Edwards' Hairstreaks you can also find ant mounds.

The Acadian Hairstreak is seen in July in wet habitats like moist meadows, marshes, and pond edges where various willows, their host plants, grow. It is rare and has only a single brood each year. It can be seen at The Nature Conservancy's Kitty Todd Preserve.

In September, when the butterfly season is coming to a close, the Oak Openings supports the Leonard's Skipper, a rare and beautiful single-brooded butterfly. It is seen in open grassy areas—such as old fields and wet meadows. The host plants for the Leonard's Skipper include various grasses.

About 50 other butterfly species can be seen in the Oak Openings region. Several are quite common and have multiple generations each year. One of these is the Eastern Tailed Blue, a very small blue butterfly, often mistaken for a Karner Blue by local land owners. It has a short tail, which the Karner lacks, and has orange spots along only the hindwing margin. One of the larval host plants is clover, which is why it is so common.

Acadian hairstreak on New Jersey Tea at Kitty Todd Nature Preserve. (Photo by Art Weber)

A second butterfly that is easily seen within the Metropark is the Spicebush Swallowtail. It is a large black butterfly with blue hindwing markings. The host plants, sassafras and spicebush, are abundant in the area. The Black Swallowtail is somewhat similar but more readily seen in backyards, as the host plants for the Black Swallowtail include parsley and dill—commonly grown in yard herb gardens.

Another very common larger butterfly within the parks is the Great Spangled Fritillary. It is bright orange with heavy black lines and spots, and white

Spicebush Swallowtail on Butterfly Milkweed at the Girdham Road sand dunes in Oak Openings Preserve Metropark. (Photo by Art Weber)

Giant Swallowtail on bergamot. (Photo by Art Weber)

triangles under the hind wing edge. It has only one generation and can be seen June thru September. The host plant is various violets that grow in open deciduous woodlands, forest margins, meadows and prairies.

The frequently-seen Viceroy is also large and orange with black veins and broad wing margins that contain two rows of small white spots. It is often confused with the Monarch Butterfly. The key to identifying the Viceroy is the thin black line that runs across the middle of the hind wings. It has two generations and the host plants include various willows and cottonwood—both plants found in wetter areas.

A third common orange and black butterfly is the Pearl Crescent. This butterfly is quite small and flies low to the ground. The larval host plant is various asters. Finally, the non-native Cabbage White Butterfly may be seen flying everywhere. It is medium-sized with multiple generations and is very successful due to its abundant host plants, members of the mustard family, which include broccoli, cabbage, and cauliflower.

Facing page: Three stages of a monarch butterfly. From left, caterpillar, chrysalis, and butterfly.
(Photos by Art Weber)

Oak Openings Dragonflies and Damselflies
By Rick Nirschl

The Oak Openings region is a wonderful location to search for dragonflies and damselflies. Sixty-nine species have been recorded in the area in the past ten years including two State of Ohio Endangered Species. To save space, here we will call them "odonates," since they belong to the insect Order Odonata.

Odonates rely on water as they spend most of their lives as aquatic creatures known as nymphs. The amount of time spent in the nymph stage varies from one or two months to as long as five or six years, depending on the species. Most species, however, mature in about eleven months. Once a nymph has matured, it will climb out of the water onto some vegetation, usually during the night, and begin the process of emerging from its exoskeleton. The head breaks through first, then the legs, and finally the wings and abdomen. This emergence usually takes about thirty minutes to an hour before the dragonfly can take its first flight.

In the Oak Openings, the two main water features are Swan Creek and its tributaries and a number of ponds, many of which are man-made and on private property.

Larvae in water can be identified but it is much easier to view these insects as adult dragonflies when they are flying during the warmer months. One of the best locations for viewing dragonflies is Wiregrass Lake on Eber Road where almost 50 species have been seen.

While odonates need water in which to lay eggs and live as larvae, once they emerge they can be found flying just about anywhere in open fields and meadows as well as near the water. Some travel a mile or more from their water source, feeding while they mature. However, once they have sexually matured, they return to the water to mate and lay eggs.

Dragonflies begin to fly in late April and continue through the summer and into November with the greatest number of species seen in June. The first species to appear are actually migrants from the south in the form of Green Darners and Swamp Darners. The abundant Green Darner is the large dragonfly you're most likely to see flying about over fields and wetlands. The first local species to hatch in late May are the state endangered Chalk-fronted Corporals along with Eastern and Fragile Forktails. Common Baskettails appear as well, and can be found flying continuous beats along roadways.

In June a wide variety of species take wing. Pronghorn and Ashy Clubtails are quite numerous, hatching both from Swan Creek and local ponds. A number of skimmers also appear in large numbers including Calico Pennants, Twelve-spotted Skimmers, Blue Dashers, and Widow Skimmers. Smaller than dragonflies, the damselflies are also putting on a show as the weather warms. Familiar, Azure, Double-striped, and Skimming Bluets are found on many ponds, along with Violet Dancers and Amber-winged Spreadwings.

Later in summer as the number of species diminishes, new species begin to appear. Some show up as migrants from the south, including Wandering and Spot-winged Gliders. These two species arrive in late July. They lay eggs, which hatch quickly into nymphs. The nymphs mature in as few as four weeks and emerge to fly south in late summer. Some of our resident species emerge here in July or August, such as Green-striped Darners and Ruby Meadowhawks. These species, along with Shadow Darners, Autumn Meadowhawks, and Spotted Spreadwings will remain active into the cool days of October.

Calico pennant dragonfly. (Photo by Rick Nirschl)

Right: A Blue-faced meadowhak.
(Photo by Rick Nirschl)

Below: A ruby meadowhawk at Wiregrass Lake Metropark.
(Photo by Art Weber)

The Antenna-Waving Wasp

A special insect of the Oak Openings is the Antenna-waving Wasp. This small wasp has an extremely patchy distribution, occurring on widely scattered sandy sites in Ohio, Michigan, Ontario, upstate New York, and the pine barrens of New Jersey. Adult wasps emerge from the soil in June. The males, tiny and black, mate with the much larger females and quickly die. Females, about one-third of an inch long, are identified by their red and black abdomens and gold-tipped antennae that are constantly waved about. They live for several weeks, during which time they hunt for juvenile grasshoppers. Finding their prey, they spring onto its back, curl their abdomens under and sting it between the segments of its thorax. The grasshopper is then paralyzed, and is dragged to a burrow the wasp had previously dug in well-packed section of sand. Dragging an animal three times its size over distances of 30 or 40 feet is a remarkable feat, but the wasp does it. A single egg is laid on the hapless grasshopper, and the burrow is closed. In this fashion a female may lay several dozen eggs in a season. In July she dies, but some of her eggs will hatch and the larval wasps consume their grasshoppers, pupate, and emerge as adults the following summer to continue the species.

I was fortunate to spend two summers helping my students carry out a research project on this little wasp. To us, their most remarkable feature is how they have persisted for thousands of years with such specialized habitat requirements. They nest only in relatively hard-packed sand—never on the soft shifting dunes. They are very weak fliers; during our studies we never saw one fly more than a few yards before landing, and never more than two feet off the ground. If their sandy patch becomes too overgrown they can no longer use it, yet they seem to have very poor dispersal abilities. Antenna-waving Wasps also have to contend with a number of predators. We saw at least one male wasp being eaten by a tiger beetle. And a small parasitic "satellite" fly follows female wasps as they drag grasshoppers to their burrows. The fly is carrying an already-hatched egg; it waits while the female wasp lays her egg on the grasshopper. When the wasp leaves, the fly enters and places its larva on the grasshopper. The fly larva then consumes the wasp's egg and the grasshopper.

Antenna-waving wasp. (Photo by Bob Jacksy)

Oak Openings Special Reptiles and Amphibians

By Kent Bekker

The Oak Openings region has many of the reptiles and amphibians that can be found throughout the county. However, three species of reptiles appear to be uniquely adapted to this region as they are not common outside of it. The Eastern Hognose Snake preys almost exclusively on toads and has evolved enlarged rear teeth and an oversized adrenal gland to allow for consumption of these toxic amphibians. The Hognose is characterized by an upturned rostral scale that gives it its common name. This scale is

Hognose snake (above) and hognose snake hacthlings (left). (Photos by Art Weber)

123

thought to assist with digging in sandy soils.

The Eastern Box Turtle is also frequently observed in the Oak Openings. Easily identified by its high-domed shell, it is Ohio's most terrestrial turtle species, and appears to be holding its own in the region. It is often seen slowly crossing roads, and is very vulnerable to being road-killed.

The Spotted Turtle is an Oak openings resident, seldom seen because of its retiring habits. It spends much time buried in wet meadows and similar damp habitats.

The widely-distributed Red-backed Salamander, mentioned in Chapter 5, is abundant in woodlands of the Oak Openings. Another interesting group of salamanders, commonly referred to as mole salamanders (Family Ambystomatidae), deserves mention. Mole salamanders spend most of their adult lives underground. They come to the surface very early in spring (sometimes in February) and migrate overland to woodland pools, where they mate and lay eggs. The eggs hatch into tadpole-like larvae, which gradually develop into air-breathing adults. These leave the pools and burrow underground until the following spring. Adult mole salamanders have remarkable homing abilities, returning over long distances to their natal pools each spring. The Tiger Salamander is the largest ambystomatid species; many other Lucas County mole salamanders are difficult to assign to species. They are genetically female and

Eastern box turtle, top. (Photo by Elliot Tramer)

A young spotted turtle, left. (Photo by Art Weber)

have multiple sets of chromosomes. A full discussion of their taxonomy is beyond the scope of this book. Metroparks volunteers visit vernal pools during evenings in early spring to monitor the populations of mole salamanders.

On mild nights in March, the Oak Openings comes alive with the calls of tiny frogs. First to emerge are the Chorus Frogs, filling standing shallow waters and ditches with calls that sound like dragging your thumb over the teeth of a comb. Soon they are joined the Spring Peepers, their high-pitched calls sounding like greatly-amplified baby chicks—a chorus of hundreds of spring peepers is an ear-splitting experience. These frogs have the remarkable ability to withstand freezing of the ditches and shallow pools they inhabit during the early spring. Later in spring, the loud calls of Gray Treefrogs replace the Chorus Frog/Spring Peeper chorus. The treefrog is one of our most beautiful animals; it has bright yellow stripes on its back legs and can change color from mottled gray to bright green. It may be heard and with luck, seen, even in suburban residential areas throughout the summer.

CHAPTER SEVEN
Lake Erie and its Wetlands

Lake Erie is the fourth-largest Great Lake in terms of surface area, being slightly larger than Lake Ontario. But in terms of volume, it is far smaller than the other Great Lakes, because it is comparatively shallow. The western basin off Lucas County is the shallowest, with an average depth of only about 30 feet. Maumee Bay, enclosed by the Woodtick Peninsula and Little Cedar Point, is even shallower. During prolonged southwest winds surface water literally gets "blown out" of the bay, reducing its depth to as little as five or six feet.

The bay receives nutrient-rich silt washing out of the Maumee River. Excessive nutrient inputs and the shallowness of the western basin are major factors in the occurrence of harmful algae blooms, discussed in Chapter 9.

A hemi-marsh at Cedar Point National Wildlife Refuge. (Photo by Art Weber)

The Annual Cycle in Lakes and Ponds

Typical temperate-zone lakes and ponds experience an annual cycle of varying oxygen and nutrient conditions. In winter, if the surface is frozen, winds cannot mix the water and nutrients sink slowly to the bottom. Algae that grew the previous summer also sink and gradually decay, removing oxygen from the water and adding additional nutrients.

In spring the ice melts and wind mixes the lake, adding oxygen to the water (by diffusion from the air) and bringing nutrients back up into the surface waters. The combination of abundant nutrients and sunlight provides ideal conditions for the growth of algae, which provide additional oxygen via photosynthesis. Also in spring, when the water is still cold, the dominant algae are usually single-celled forms called diatoms. But as the lake continues to warm and more nutrients enter from the surrounding land, slimy mats of "blue-green algae" (actually cyanobacteria) may form. By mid-summer, the lake stratifies, forming two distinct layers. The surface layer is warm and has lots of algae and adequate oxygen. The deep layer is colder; dead materials accumulate and decay there and oxygen concentrations may be low.

In the western basin of Lake Erie, the normal annual cycle is different. Because the basin is wide but very shallow, winds can easily churn up the water, continually bringing water from the bottom back to the surface. Ice cover during winter cold periods does allow materials to sink, but in summer the western basin stratifies weakly, if at all. Nutrients that would remain near the bottom in a stratified lake are continuously being resuspended in western Lake Erie, fueling blooms of blue-green algae.

The Lake Erie Fishery

The high productivity of algae in the lake provides a base for a very rich food pyramid. The energy captured by algae is transferred to tiny invertebrate animals (zooplankton) that feed on the algae, then on up the food chain to the fish. For more than 100 years, Lake Erie supported one of the world's largest fresh water fisheries. Through much of the twentieth century, the commercial fishery brought about 50 million pounds of fish to market each year. This represented about half of the commercial fish catch from the entire Great Lakes. Originally, the dominant species taken were Lake Whitefish, Sauger, Cisco, and Blue Pike. But water quality in the lake was steadily deteriorating and stocks of those species were being depleted by overfishing. By the 1960s populations of all four species had collapsed (see charts), and the commercial fishery had to turn to species of lower market value, such as Walleye, Yellow Perch, Smelt, and Carp. By the 1970s overfishing and pollution had reduced the numbers of Walleye, and contamination of Walleye flesh by mercury—a toxic heavy metal in coal-fired power plant effluents—caused a temporary ban on Walleye fishing. Subsequently numbers of Walleye recovered, although today the Lake Erie fishery remains less productive than it was a century ago. Walleye and Yellow Perch remain the most common species taken by Lake Erie fishermen.

Collapse of Lake Erie Fishery

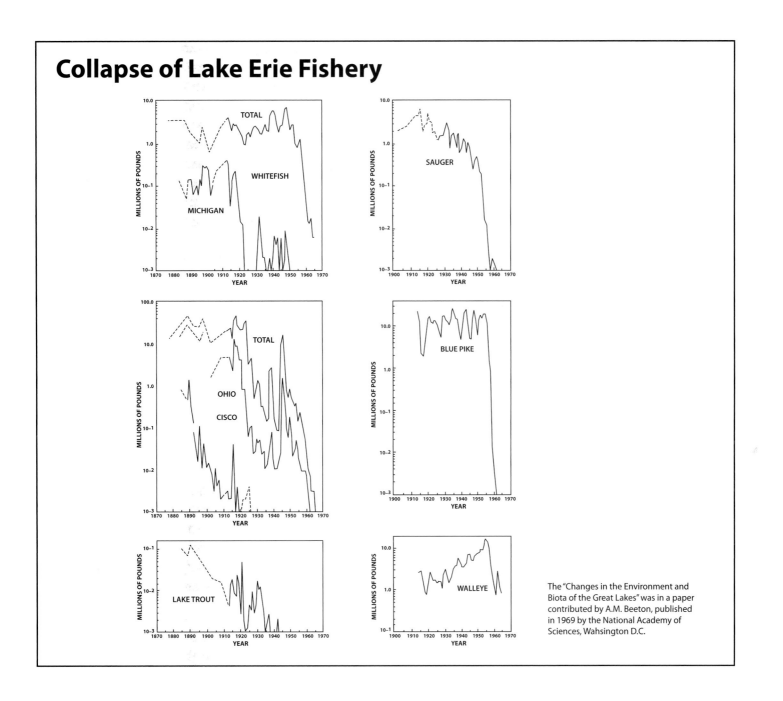

The "Changes in the Environment and Biota of the Great Lakes" was in a paper contributed by A.M. Beeton, published in 1969 by the National Academy of Sciences, Wahsington D.C.

The "Canadian Soldier" Mayflies Return

Growing up in northern Ohio, my brothers and I eagerly awaited a magical day in June when the "Canadian soldiers" appeared. It was an annual event, anticipated with disgust by the grown-ups but an enchanting spectacle for us kids. On that magical day, we awoke to find our window screens so covered with "soldiers" that we couldn't see out. We dashed outside to enjoy the spectacle. They were everywhere. The sidewalks were covered; we squashed dozens with every step. They landed on our clothes, in our hair, even in our mouths if we weren't careful. We cheered each time a car skidded on their slippery bodies, careening through the stop sign and into the intersection at the end of our street. Soon

the street sweeping machines came, piling the "soldiers" knee deep on the curbs, blocking the storm drains. If there was rain that day, the streets flooded. After a few days they disappeared, though the stench of their decaying bodies lingered.

Then, in 1954, a strange thing happened. The massive invasions stopped. Years later, I learned that "Canadian soldiers" were the adult form of a large mayfly, *Hexagenia limbata*, that lays its eggs over the waters of Lake Erie. The eggs sink, and soon hatch into young nymphs that feed on dead materials on the lake bottom. Two years (usually) later, they swim to the surface, shed their skins, and emerge in vast mating flights of adult mayflies. If there is a north wind, billions of them are carried ashore into our towns. But the late summer and fall of 1953 were

Mayfly nymph.
(Photo by Art Weber)

unusually hot and calm. For the first time ever, oxygen levels along the bottom of Lake Erie dropped to near zero, suffocating most of the mayfly nymphs. Even the western basin was becalmed.

That was many years ago, and as the condition of Lake Erie gradually improved in the 1980s, oxygen levels began to rise and areas near the lake began to experience June mayfly swarms again. This improvement was largely achieved by removing phosphates from laundry detergents and adopting better methods of municipal sewage treatment. Both reduced the amounts of algae-feeding nutrients entering the lake.

The recovery of the mayfly is a hopeful sign, but I wonder whether the huge mayfly emergences occurred in pioneer days, when the lake was clean enough to drink. The few accounts of this area written in the early 1800s do not mention them. Perhaps the swarms of the 1940s were an early warning sign that the lake was becoming too enriched—and eventually when enrichment became so severe that it depleted the oxygen, even the mayflies couldn't withstand it.

An adult mayfly. (Photo by Art Weber)

The Lake Erie Marshes

When the first European settlers came to this area in the 1700s, a band of wetlands several miles wide extended from Sandusky Bay around the western end of Lake Erie all the way to the mouth of the Detroit River. Changes in the water level of the lake dictated the water regime of the marshes; strong northeast winds created seiches (oscillations in water level) that drove water far inland, and when the wind blew from the southwest the waters retreated lakeward. Early accounts tell us that Maumee Bay was filled with emergent vegetation taller than a man's head—much of it wild rice, now rare in our area. Today most of the original wetlands have been drained and converted to some of world's richest farmland. Maumee Bay has become an expanse of open water, devoid of emergent plants. The remaining wetlands—perhaps five percent of their original size—are less responsive to water levels of the lake, since most are enclosed within dikes. Most of today's marshes are managed by pumps and gates that can be opened and closed, allowing water levels inside the impoundments to be raised or lowered according to management needs. A few, such as Metzger Marsh, have been reconnected with Lake Erie to allow fish and other organisms to move freely back and forth.

State and federal agency ownership of the lake-

Facing page: Sunset at Howard Marsh, one of the many wetlands in Lucas County. (Photo by Art Weber)

Right: An American Coot at Howard Marsh Metropark. The bird is known by thousands of people by its other name, the Mud Hen. (Photo by Art Weber)

shore marshes dates from the mid-twentieth century. Until the 1940s, most of the marshes that still existed were owned by private sportsmen's clubs and used primarily for waterfowl hunting. Bird watchers, hunters, and others who enjoy the marshes today owe a great debt to these far-sighted sportsmen, whose ownership prevented the marshes from being converted either to marinas or dry land developments.

Although these wetlands represent only a tiny fraction of what existed here in pioneer days, the surviving marshes constitute probably the largest and most important wetland complex in the Great Lakes region. Fortunately, in recent years the conversion of lakeshore wetlands to agricultural fields has been reversed. Some large parcels with a long history of remaining wet late into the spring have been sold to the U.S. Fish & Wildlife Service, Metroparks Toledo, or the Ohio Division of Wildlife and are being converted back to wetlands. Examples include Howard Farms and half of Pearson Metropark.

Dominant plants in the marshes include giant reed, narrowleaf cattail, lotus, various smartweeds (*Polygonum species*) and flowering rush. Some of these dominants are non-native invaders from Europe or Asia. Purple loosestrife is another non-native invader of little wildlife value, which is being controlled for the most part by aerial spraying of herbicides and introduced beetles. More on these invasive wetland plants can be found in Chapter 9.

Purple loosestrife, an invasive marsh plant.
(Photo by Art Weber)

On the dikes, gray dogwood is the dominant shrub; its berries provide excellent food for birds in the fall. Common trees bordering the wetlands include black willow, cottonwood, and boxelder.

Among the mammals, Muskrats are very important marsh engineers. Their activities have a profound influence on the pattern of marsh vegetation. Muskrats harvest emergent plants—especially cattails—for food and for constructing their lodges. Their removal of large clusters of cattails creates a patchwork of emergent vegetation and open pools (the "hemi-marsh") that provides ideal habitat structure for marsh birds and other animal life. Minks are common predators in the marshes, and feed on Muskrats and a variety of smaller animals.

A muskrat (above) and multiple muskrat cabins at Cedar Point National Wildlife Refuge (left). (Photos by Art Weber)

135

A mink, a primary predator of muskrats.
(Photo by Art Weber)

Birds of the Lake Erie Marshes

The marshes along the southwest flank of Lake Erie and the adjacent waters of the lake constitute one of the most important waterfowl staging areas in North America. Ducks and Tundra Swans migrating between their summer homes in the far north and wintering areas to the south stop to feed in the productive waters of the marshes and the lake's western basin. Peak times for the passage of waterfowl through our area are March-April in spring and late October into December in the fall. If the waters of the lake remain open, large numbers of ducks and geese will stay through the winter.

Here are some examples of estimated waterfowl numbers from our area: In 2011, over 2,000 Tundra Swans remained at Cedar Point National Wildlife Refuge through mid-December. In the marshes, Gadwalls and Mallards frequently number in the thousands. In mid-April 2014, an estimated 94,000 scaup—mostly Lesser Scaup—covered the surface of Maumee Bay. Aerial surveys of waterfowl by the

Ohio Division of Wildlife have produced counts of well over 200,000 ducks on the lake. Surveys at Cedar Point National Wildlife Refuge by members of the Toledo Naturalists' Association sometimes produce counts of nearly 100,000 waterfowl (ducks, geese and swans) during spring and fall migration.

The marshes also serve as vital nesting and feeding areas for America's national bird, the Bald Eagle. In 1970, only four pairs of Bald Eagles nested in Ohio, and their eggs often failed to hatch due to

Short eared owl at Magee Marsh Wildlife Area.
(Photo by Art Weber)

A Black-necked Stilt on its nest at Howard Marsh Metropark.
(Photo by Art Weber)

heavy burdens of dichlorodiphenyltrichloroethane (DDT) and other insecticides that prevented female eagles from depositing enough calcium to make strong eggshells. After the banning of DDT in 1972, eagle populations gradually recovered. In 2018 there were 286 pairs of eagles nesting in Ohio, producing 445 young. The shore of Lake Erie may have more nesting Bald Eagles than anywhere else in the U.S. outside of Alaska. The Lake Erie wetlands are also an important fall staging area for eagles. Bird counts at Cedar Point National Wildlife Refuge have yielded as many as 47 eagles in a single morning. The recovery

Facing page: A bald eagle and its nest. (Photo by Art Weber)

Great Blue heron on the icy Maumee River near Farnsworth Metropark.
(Photo by Art Weber)

Egrets at Weir Rapids below Bendview Metropark.
(Photo by Art Weber)

of the Bald Eagle is a great success story in wildlife conservation.

Each May, the lakeshore provides yet another avian spectacle. Songbirds migrating northward from their winter homes in the American tropics, hesitant to strike out across the open waters of Lake Erie, often "pile up" in woodlots along the south shore. On favorable weather days, the numbers of birds thronging these small woodlots can virtually overwhelm the senses of visiting bird watchers. The "fallout" of migrants along the lakeshore occurs at a time when huge numbers of aquatic insects—mostly midges—are emerging from the waters of the lake and adjacent marshes. The result is a feeding bonanza for the birds, many of them famished and exhausted from their long flights. The "stars" of the show are the small, colorful wood warblers, but over 100 species of birds can be found at a single lakeshore location on a good May morning.

The prime spot to view this phenomenon is the Magee Marsh "Bird Trail," a boardwalk that traverses a seven-acre woodlot behind the beach—but be

Photographers on the bird trail at Magee Marsh Wildlife Area.
(Photo by Art Weber)

prepared to share the area with several thousand other birders.

The spectacular spring migration along the Lake Erie shore has become an annual pilgrimage for birders far and wide, thanks in part to the "Biggest Week in American Birding," sponsored by the Black Swamp Bird Observatory. At this writing it is the largest birding festival in North America; it takes place during the second week of May each year and is headquartered at the lodge in Maumee Bay State Park in eastern Lucas County.

A yellow warbler (above) and a chestnut-sided warbler (left).
(Photos by Art Weber)

141

Above: Trumpeter Swans at Howard Marsh Metropark. (Photo by Art Weber)

Right: A red-breasted Merganser on the Maumee River near Audobon Island and Side Cut Metropark. (Photo by Art Weber)

Dragonflies and Damselflies of the Lake Erie Shoreline and Marshes

By Rick Nirschl

A strong southerly wind in mid to late April can deposit many early migrating birds to the woodlot at Metzger Marsh, and that same wind can sometimes also bring dragonflies along with them. Green Darners and Swamp Darners ride these winds and like the birds are reluctant to cross Lake Erie. They then gather along the lakeshore feeding, sometimes in large swarms. Most, if not all, of these darners likely emerged in the southern states before migrating north.

The marshes at Metzger and Magee don't have the diversity of dragonflies one can find in the Oak Openings, but they make up for that with large numbers of a few species. There are times in June when there are thousands of Blue Dashers on the beach at Magee. A single dead sumac might be adorned with thirty Blue Dashers, and as you walk along huge clouds of dashers, and later Autumn Meadowhawks, billow up in front of you. Black Saddlebags, Wandering Gliders, and Green Darners add to the spectacle.

Dragonflies and damselflies are predators and are drawn to the abundant insects on the beaches and marshes of Lake Erie. They feed on any insect they can overpower, from tiny flies and mosquitoes up to large insects including butterflies and other

A female Blue Dasher dragonfly. Blue Dashers are abundant in lakeshore marshes. (Photo by Rick Nirschl)

dragonflies. Eastern Pondhawks are commonly seen eating other dragonflies. On the other hand, dragonflies are prey to other species. Birds, spiders and robber flies all feed on dragonflies, especially when they are young ("teneral") and have just emerged.

The woodlot at Metzger is a great place to find Vesper Bluets when a south wind pushes this damselfly out of the marshes and into the woodlot and vegetation along the shore. These bluets mix with Slender Spreadwings and Skimming Bluets, among others.

In August 2006, the first state record Striped Saddlebags was found at Metzger Marsh and a few days later three more were found at Magee. This long-distance traveler is a south Texas species that occasionally wanders north. This species has been found at Magee several times since this first sighting but has only been seen once in one other Ohio location in Lake County.

Activity slows down a bit in July and August but picks up again in September when Green-striped Darners begin to emerge. Soon after, the southward migration begins with Green Darners and Black Saddlebags forming large swarms along the beaches. The dragonflies are migrating south but stop to feed in the marshes and when a strong south wind blows, they are pushed to the lakeshore in swarms that sometimes number in the hundreds. These migrants will fly to southern states where they will lay eggs to form a new population that will migrate north in the spring.

Reptiles of the Lakeshore Marshes
By Kent Bekker

The Lake Erie marshes are home to several reptiles unique to this region. The Eastern Fox Snake is an obvious example; it is distributed along the western basin of Lake Erie, appearing equally well-adapted to the marsh and shoreline. The melanistic form of the Eastern Garter Snake is also a unique member of near-shore habitats. Although the Garter Snake is not restricted to this area, there must be some selection process causing the melanistic form to

Painted turtles sunning themselves on a log at Magee Marsh Wildlife Area. (Photo by Art Weber)

comprise a high proportion of the population in the marshes. Most of the snakes residing in the Lake Erie wetlands appear to reach higher densities than elsewhere in the region. In appropriate (warm) weather many snakes of multiple species can easily be observed.

Turtles are very conspicuous in the marshes, basking in the sun to raise their body temperatures. One species, the Blanding's Turtle, remains readily observable in the marshes, while it has declined through much of the rest of its range. The Blanding's Turtle is frequently seen basking in early spring, when temperatures are still cool. It can be distinguished from the more abundant Painted Turtle by its higher-domed shell and bright yellow throat.

The Future is Bright

The future is bright for the Great Lakes region. Over the past 50 years, the U.S. population has shifted southward. States like Arizona, California, Texas, and Florida have grown tremendously, whereas Midwestern states like Ohio have lost population.

But water shortages have become almost routine in the southwest and pose a future threat in Florida as well. Continued growth in much of the south may be water-limited. But we have abundant water—more than twenty percent of the world's surface fresh water is in our Great Lakes. While other regions face shortages, our region can flourish, if we protect the quality of our precious waters.

CHAPTER EIGHT

The Lake, the Maumee, and its Tributaries

The Maumee is the largest river entering the Great Lakes. It forms at Fort Wayne, Indiana and flows northeastward, entering the southwest corner of Lake Erie at Toledo, in Lucas County. The drainage basin includes most of northwest Ohio, a portion of northeast Indiana, and a small area of southeastern Michigan. Much of the river's watershed is intensively farmed. Fields are generally tile-drained to speed the flow of water into ditches, which drain into creeks, and eventually into the river. Thus, the Maumee and its tributaries carry heavy loads of suspended silt, often giving them a muddy appearance.

Major creek systems in Lucas County include the Ottawa River and Swan Creek. The Ottawa arises from tributaries in the northwest portion of the county (including Tenmile Creek) and flows east-

The interurban bridge over the muddy Maumee River. (Photo courtesy *The Blade*, David Patch, 2019)

ward, entering directly into Maumee Bay – north of the mouth of the Maumee and north of the Ohio-Michigan state line. Swan Creek drains the southwest portion of the county, flows eastward through Toledo, and enters the Maumee River south of the city center. A curious fact is that Swan Creek originally flowed through downtown and entered the river farther north, but its flow was diverted in 1921.

The following essay by Dr. Todd Crail on flowing waters also revisits conditions in Lake Erie, as influenced by the flow of rivers into Maumee Bay. The interconnectedness of our bodies of water, and the lake's dependence on the conditions in our rivers, made it essential to revisit Lake Erie in this chapter.

The Waters of Lucas County
By Dr. Todd Crail

The waters of Lucas County are perhaps our most misunderstood and least appreciated natural resource. As a young man, I spent many hours fishing the Maumee River and exploring the banks of Swan Creek. I often found myself thinking, "I wish I could have seen this before it was all screwed up." That changed for me in May 1997. I'd been challenged by an ichthyologist acquaintance to not assume there were only carp, catfish and a few lonely Smallmouth Bass in these streams, aside from the times when Walleye and White Bass wandered in from the lake. I bought a cheap seine net and dragged a buddy to Tenmile Creek near Northview High School. We were told to try a technique called "darter dance" where

you place the net downstream and kick the rocks to flush small fish living there into the net. We did this, and when we lifted the net, we found magic. In the net were a half dozen nuptial male Orangethroat Darters adorned in swaths of bright azure and hot orange. Since I had blindly passed over such magnificent creatures for years, it is understandable that many people mistakenly perceive our waterways as waste areas that are a liability to our economy and wellbeing.

Lake Erie is now a headline topic in the water quality crisis resulting from nutrient-fueled harmful algal blooms. A considerable proportion of the nutrients fueling the bloom are fed into the lake through the Maumee River, resulting from agricultural, sewage and landscaping practices. Perhaps most influential in shaping the public's opinion are the fine sediments carried by our streams, literally "muddying" our perception of these resources, just as my own view had been shaped.

Without question, the waters of Lucas County have been degraded; something has been lost. Aquatic degradation arises from seemingly minor choices made across the landscape that add up and accumulate in our rivers and magnify in Maumee Bay. Every citizen in our region contributes, myself included. In many conversations about the lake's issues, the finger of blame is pointed at farmers, yet they are only delivering a product that consumers demand at the lowest possible price. The problem is everyone, yet no individual in particular. And yet, as the Orangethroat Darters revealed, a rich and beautiful fauna persists in our waterways.

A pod of pelicans alight from the Maumee River near Roche de Bout. Pelicans have one of the largest wingspans of any bird in North America. (Photo by Art Weber)

If we knew about the rich life in our waterways, and what is still possible, would we make different choices? Would we be willing to pay extra to prevent their pollution? Our waters are a resource worthy of celebration rather than disgrace, and it is worth the effort to understand why our waters are degraded and take the necessary steps to improve them.

The waters of Lucas County are globally significant

By surface area, Lake Erie is the thirteenth largest body of water in the world, a part of the Great Lakes, which hold twenty percent of the world's fresh water. Allow these facts to sink in. I often tell my students that they live in a region set to prosper in light of changing climate, so long as we do not degrade our resources beyond use before the world wants them.

Lake Erie's western basin is the "fishiest" of all the Great Lakes. Because of its shallow depth, warm climate and a historically moderate amount of nutrients coming from the watershed, the ecological productivity of the western basin is unparalleled among the five Great Lakes, and globally rivaled in biomass only by great lake systems in Africa. The shallow depth of the lake is also one of its greatest advantages. Although this feature makes it easy to pollute because of its comparatively small volume, it also has a flushing time of two-and-a-half years. That is, on average, any drop of water entering the lake will

leave in two-and-a-half years. Therefore, the lake is able to heal itself quickly if the source of a pollution problem is removed.

The Maumee River accounts for about twenty percent of the discharge to Lake Erie's western basin (the Detroit River contributes nearly 80 percent); the Maumee's average discharge is about 45,000 cubic feet per second, although this varies widely with rainfall and snow melt conditions. Perhaps more important, the Maumee contributes over 50 percent of Lake Erie's total sediment load. The Maumee's heavy inputs of phosphorus and nitrogen are major contributors to the large amounts of algal biomass produced each year in the western basin, although sewage and other pollutants entering from the Detroit River are also significant.

The western basin and its tributary streams are among the most productive and biologically diverse of great lake systems in the northern hemisphere. For example, there are over 100 fish species native to the western basin watershed, nearly all of which have been historically recorded within Lucas County, and which decrease in number as you head north and west. For comparison, the entire Columbia River watershed hosts 33 native species of fish; the Colorado River has only 25. Part of our high diversity stems from the mixing of northern and southern communities. Lake Erie is connected to the deeper, colder Great Lakes to the north, and receives inputs from warmer rivers flowing up from the south. Thus,

An osprey with a fish at Side Cut Metropark. (Photo by Art Weber)

fish representative of both northern and southern aquatic communities meet in western Lake Erie, and in the waters of the Maumee River. Our small streams are also surprisingly diverse. Despite human activities such as damming, ditching and dredging, a surprising amount of biodiversity persists. For example, in a drainage ditch in western Lucas County, I have observed 27 fish species that are able to occupy this ephemeral (intermittent-flowing) system due to its connections to larger, more stable waterbodies downstream.

We can learn much from the recent history of our aquatic resources

Historically, Lake Erie fisheries were dominated by species that required clean, cold water and are now primarily found in the upper Great Lakes. Between 1885 and 1924, "Lake Herring," primarily the Cisco, catches varied between 13 and 48 million pounds per year. However, stocks plummeted to 5.6 million pounds in 1925 and continued to decline thereafter. The 1937 catch was only 1,500 pounds, and Cisco is now listed as endangered by the Ohio Division of Wildlife (DOW).

Lake Sturgeon are large—up to seven feet—prehistoric-looking fish that have inhabited North American waters for millions of years and were once common in Lake Erie. Early soldier accounts tell of sturgeon spawning aggregations in the rapids of the Maumee River that were dense enough to walk "across their backs." They were caught, dried and used as fire wood at Fort Meigs. Not only were Lake

Sturgeon abundant, but so were other valued species such as Muskellunge, Northern Pike, and Walleye. An observer in 1815 remarked "So numerous are they at this place, that a spear may be thrown into the water at random and will rarely miss killing one!"

Certainly, overharvest influenced the demise of these species. Lake Sturgeon are nearly absent from the state and listed as endangered by the DOW. The last known Muskellunge from the Maumee River was caught in 1959. As fishery after fishery crashed, people switched to species with life history traits that allowed their numbers to soar in the absence of the larger, longer-lived species, and were tolerant to changing habitat conditions. Walleye stocks expanded, peaking in 1956 with a lake-wide commercial harvest reaching fifteen million pounds, but crashed to 160,000 pounds by 1966. Smallmouth Bass numbers soared in the Maumee River. Lou Campbell, a local bird expert and avid fisherman, recounted that he and a partner caught 124 Smallmouth each in a single day of fishing the rapids of the Maumee sometime in the late 1950s. However, he lamented their virtual disappearance by 1970. Human-induced changes to the lake and rivers have largely prevented recovery after a species' population crashes.

In the late nineteenth and early twentieth centuries, heavy sediment loads resulting from land use conversion to agriculture suppressed the richness and abundance of fish species in many streams. This factor alone has played a major role in the impairment of aquatic communities and removed a handful of sediment-intolerant species by the turn of the twentieth century. The commercially important Lake Herring was lost from Maumee Bay, and non-game species, most notably, the Gilt Darter and the now-extinct Harelip Sucker, were extirpated from the Maumee. It is important to note that each had narrow habitat requirements and were also on the northern or southern edges of their range. It also is important to note that most other species were able to maintain a presence well into the 1940s and 1950s, many of which expanded their abundance. So sediment could not be the only culprit.

Part of the historic land conversion involved the practices of straightening of stream channels, removing woody debris, draining wetlands, building dams, and encroaching on stream flood plains. These activities have three profound consequences that are critical for understanding the story of aquatic resources in Lucas County.

First, these practices cause a loss of potential habitats. Free-flowing rivers manage their energy through bends and curves, sediment bars that create riffles and pools, and varying amounts of woody debris, especially in an area of such low topographical relief as Lucas County. Each structural component hosts species that specifically use that feature as habitat; for example, the Dusky Darter favors woody debris and undercut tree roots in flowing pools, where they have the curious habit of grazing upside down on insect larvae "hiding" on the bottom of the wood; the Sand Darter favors silt-free sand bars, in which they can quickly vibrate and bury themselves from predators; or the Spotted Gar, who lives among heavily vegetated runs and pools, from where they ambush their prey. Without these distinct habitat features, these species are quickly lost.

Second, the accelerated velocity of a straightened river has more energy to mobilize sediment (erosion). The streams become muddier, warmer, maintain less regular flow and flood more quickly. Each of these differences can exceed the tolerances of species, displacing them from the community. But the river will also heal itself through erosion. The stream first cuts downward into the river bed, then undercuts the banks, causing the banks to slump into the channel, along with trees that line the bank. Most people would view this process as detrimental, but it is necessary, and in many cases beneficial to the organisms living in the stream (sheet erosion off agricultural fields and construction sites is a different matter).

The in-fall helps the stream begin to manage its energy, which in time, reduces the amount of fine sediment, increases the residence time of water, and reduces downstream flooding. The process happens most rapidly in young stream channels but is ongoing even in mature streams. New local habitats are created by holes and woody debris; existing downstream habitats are rejuvenated with sand and gravel. Think how these processes are required by Dusky and Sand Darters, or by the seemingly unimpressive group of "bottom feeders," collectively known as the suckers (Catastomidae), one of my favorite fish families.

A third consequence of stream modification is the lost ability of the river to process nutrients (Nitrogen and Phosphorus) on its floodplain. By dissecting the river from the floodplain, the system has become separated from its primary filtering and cleansing mechanism, much like cutting out a person's liver, reducing up to 90 percent of a river's ability to regulate the important geochemical cycles of N and P. This reduction has profound implications for downstream systems, as they receive a proverbial "fire hose" of these nutrients, leading to downstream ecological phenomena such as toxic algae blooms, which can render water undrinkable for humans.

The Maumee River suffered a devastating blow in the winter of 1960-61 when low flow and thick ice allowed urban sewage effluents to "winter kill" most of the river, sparing only Common Carp and Bullhead Catfish.

Dawn at Weir rapids, just downstream from Bendview Metropark.
(Photo by Art Weber)

The culmination of many years of stream and lake degradation occurred in the 1960s, with the collapse of the major portion of Lake Erie's commercial fishery, the infamous burning of the Cuyahoga River in Cleveland, and the declaration in news articles and popular books that Lake Erie was "dead." In truth, the lake was hardly "dead;" it was teeming with life. Enrichment of the waters had produced abundant life of undesirable kinds—excessive blue-green algae blooms, bacterial populations dense enough to close swimming beaches, and low-value fish species adapted to polluted waters.

Positive changes began in the 1970s, with the passage of the Clean Water Act. Improvements have included the removal of Phosphorus from laundry detergents, the replacement of many leaking septic systems and urban combined sewer overflows, the removal of dams from tributary streams, better containment of landfills, and a conservation reserve program (unfortunately not renewed) to pay farmers for putting fields aside for a season to provide wildlife habitat and reduce nutrient runoff into streams.

Lake Erie is still the "fishiest" of all the Great Lakes. In 2015 the catch of Walleye, Yellow Perch, Smallmouth Bass, and White Bass and other species added up to 4.3 million fish taken in the Ohio waters of Lake Erie, much of it caught in the western basin. Catches of Largemouth Bass and Northern Pike have recently surged. This pattern is most likely in response to the invasion of Ponto Caspian mussels (Zebra and Quagga), which seem to have encouraged expansion of visual predator populations by clearing the water and providing plant cover from which to strike.

Today, the bounty of the river is celebrated each spring by hundreds of fishermen who come to catch spawning Walleye and White Bass along the rapids of the Maumee. I have personally experienced ag-

Facing page: A view from the Jefferson Avenue bridge in Cleveland of the Cuyahoga River fire, November 3, 1952. (Photo courtesy the Cleveland Press Collection at Cleveland State University Library)

Right: A Walleye.

gregations of Walleye so dense that one cannot help but trip or step on the fish. Many fishermen return later in the season to angle for Smallmouth Bass and Channel and Flathead Catfish. As Chapter 9 makes clear, much remains to be done; but, we have come a long way since the days when Lake Erie and its tributaries we used as receptacles for our waste, with no thought to the consequences.

Dragonflies and Damselflies of the Maumee River
By Rick Nirschl

Side Cut, Farnsworth, and Providence Metroparks are all good locations to look for dragonflies and damselflies that are unique to the Maumee River. Search for them along the shoreline, but also

Spring 2019 walleye run.
(Photo by Art Weber)

look for them perching in vegetation away from the water in meadows and along paths.

The first species to emerge in early June are the clubtails. Midland Clubtail is the most likely to be found, while Cobra and Plains Clubtails are more rare. The Plains is a State Endangered Species. They all can be found perching on rocks along the shore or flying low over the river in search of food. These are impressive creatures with bold markings and coloration and have large clubs on the tip of the abdomen.

Later in June and into July, damselflies begin to emerge. American Rubyspots, Stream Bluets, Blue-fronted Dancers, and Powdered Dancers can be found at multiple locations along the river. There is a healthy population of Rainbow Bluets along the Siegert Lake shoreline at Side Cut and another along the canal at Providence Metropark. American Rubyspots can easily be found along the banks of the Maumee River at Farnsworth Metropark. Dragon-

Left: Cobra Clubtail. (Photo by Rick Nirschl)

Below: Plains Clubtail. (Photo by Rick Nirschl)

Bottom Left: American Rubyspot. (Photo by Tom Sheehan)

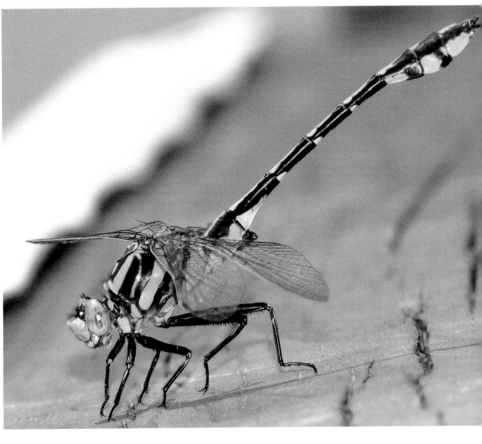

flies flying at this time would include Black Saddlebags, Common Whitetails, and Eastern Amberwings.

In August another clubtail, the Flag-tailed Spinyleg, emerges and can be found along the shoreline, especially at Farnsworth Metropark. This is more of a western species and is generally only found in the western portions of Ohio. It is a truly impressive dragonfly with a large rust-colored club.

Also flying in August are the river cruisers. These might be even more impressive than the clubtails. They are large, around three and a half inches, are boldly marked in black and yellow and have beautiful bright green eyes that look like beacons as they fly patrols in the meadows of the parks. Swift River Cruiser is our most common species with the Roy-

al River Cruiser a close second. Gilded River Cruisers are more scarce, and we have another puzzling cruiser called the Wabash River Cruiser. It may be a hybrid of the Royal and Gilded River Cruisers.

Native Mussels
By Dr. Todd Crail

Lake Erie and the streams of Lucas County support a surprising variety of native mussels, known to specialists as unionids, because they belong to the mollusc Family Unionidae. Some species are quite small, but others may grow shells up to 10 inches (25 cm) across. Most adult mussels are filter-feeders, collecting algae from the water column using their siphons and particles of organic matter from the substrate using their foot. Most live partially buried in the bottom sediments while some are completely buried their entire lives. Where they are numerous, they are important ecosystem engineers, transferring filtered materials from the water column to the sediments. These materials can later be returned to the open waters to provide nutrients for growth of algae and bacteria, completing the cycle.

Unionid molluscs have a fascinating life history. Their larvae are semi-parasitic on fish, especially members of the group that includes sunfish, bass, and perch. The mussel larvae, called glochidia, apparently do not harm their hosts unless attached to the gills in very large numbers, effectively suffocating the fish. The glochidia transform into juvenile mussels while attached to the fish, which takes three to four weeks. After they have transformed, they drop off the fish into the substrate which allows mussels to disperse to new habitats, should the fish move to a different section of the stream.

The females of some species have modified tissues to attract fish to nibble them; their patterns and behavior look like crawling crayfish, Dobson fly larvae, or swimming minnows. When a fish bites, the females send out glochidia, which attach to the gills of the fish. Other species have packets of glochidia called conglutinates that look like a small worm or larval fish, which prompts fish to bite, forcing an explosion of glochidia in the fishes' mouth. One group of mussels, known as the combshells, actually grabs their fish host as the fish rummage through the substrate.

A few Lucas County mussels are considered quite rare. For example, the Rayed Bean, which lives in some sections of Swan Creek, has been added to the federal Endangered Species List by the U.S. Department of the Interior. Our two combshell species, the Snuffbox and Northern Riffleshell, have become extirpated from our county (both are also listed as federally endangered). Populations of species remnant in the creeks and rivers of the county are holding their own, but most species have dramatically declined in Maumee Bay and western Lake Erie. This is primarily due to invasions by the Eurasian Zebra and Quagga Mussels, which have taken over much of the substrate, compete with native mussels for food, and may even encrust their shells so heavily that native mussels are unable to feed or respire. More will be said about these invaders in Chapter 9.

CHAPTER NINE

Conservation Challenges

To ensure that our rich natural inheritance will be here for future generations, we must attend to several challenges. Currently, the primary issues of concern in our area are habitat loss, degraded water quality causing toxic algae "blooms," and invasive species.

Habitat Loss

Despite a slowly declining human population, the amount of developed land in Lucas County has nearly doubled in the past 50 years. Farms and woodlands have been converted to residential developments, commercial strips, and shopping malls. Soils that once absorbed rain water have been paved over; vegetation that once provided wildlife

Algae in Lake Erie at Maumee Bay State Park. (Photo courtesy *The Blade,* Katie Rausch, 2014)

cover has been cleared. The additive effects of these conversions is that high-diversity biological communities have been replaced by low-diversity biological communities, dominated by a comparatively small number of species adapted to human disturbance.

Fortunately, many people feel that the aesthetic value of these high-diversity communities is reason enough to preserve them. But there is more at stake than the loss of species of purely aesthetic or academic interest. The natural habitats that support a diversity of wildlife also provide us with vital ecological services, free of charge. Cities are not ecologically self-sustaining. Most of the resources used in the city—food, pure water, construction materials, fuels, minerals—must come from elsewhere, i.e., from the countryside. In addition, cities produce vast amounts of waste in the form of sewage, air pollutants, industrial wastes, garbage, carbon dioxide, and heat. Some of these wastes are treated to reduce their toxicity, but in the end they are exported from the city to the countryside, which must absorb and cleanse them. In other words, a healthy landscape cannot be entirely "developed;" it must include sufficient clean water, clean air, and vegetation to absorb the effluents of our society. Finally, recent research has shown that people are happier and healthier living in landscapes that provide abundant opportunities to experience nature.

The ratio of developed to undeveloped land that will ensure a healthy landscape is an important question but possibly unanswerable; for one thing, it will be different for every region. But we can be certain that the more natural habitat we can provide, the better. Parks, preserves and wildlife refuges are crucial to this effort, but private property owners can make significant contributions as well by planting their own yards in native flowers, shrubs and trees. Helpful ideas about how this may be accomplished can be found in a variety of sources, but a good place to start is the Nature Conservancy's recent publication, *Living in the Oak Openings*.

Harmful Algal Blooms in Western Lake Erie
By Dr. Tom Bridgeman

For two days in August 2014, nearly half a million residents in the Toledo area were informed that they should not use their tap water for drinking or bathing. The reason? A harmful algal bloom (HAB) caused by microscopic blue-green algae called *Microcystis* had produced large amounts of a potent toxin in Lake Erie—the city's source for drinking water. The toxin temporarily overwhelmed the Toledo water treatment plant's defenses and entered the drinking water supply. The treatment plant staff quickly doubled their toxin-removal measures and safe water was restored, but not before causing a near-panic and millions of dollars in economic damage to the area.

Problems with HABs in Lake Erie have a long history. In the 1960s and 1970s, pollution and HABs in Lake Erie brought national attention to the lake. The Cuyahoga River leading to the lake was so polluted that it frequently caught on fire and Lake Erie was declared "dead." The silver lining to Lake Erie's problems was that it spurred a national environ-

Toledo's water intake crib in Lake Erie. (Photo courtesy *The Blade*, Dave Zapotosky, 2014)

mental movement. The U.S. Environmental Protection Agency was formed, the Clean Water Act was passed, and the U.S. and Canadian governments agreed to clean up the Great Lakes by restricting the release of pollutants into the lake. From the late 1970s through the mid-1990s, Lake Erie's waters became steadily cleaner and HABs became a thing of the past. Therefore, when HABs began to return in the late 1990s and grew worse each year everyone

was confused. Didn't we already solve the problems in Lake Erie? What went wrong?

When scientists think about the causes of harmful algal blooms, they mainly think about phosphorus and nitrogen. These two elements are important ingredients in commercial fertilizers that help lawns and farm crops grow. Algae behaves just like green plants, depending on nitrogen and phosphorus in the water to grow. A little algae is good—it

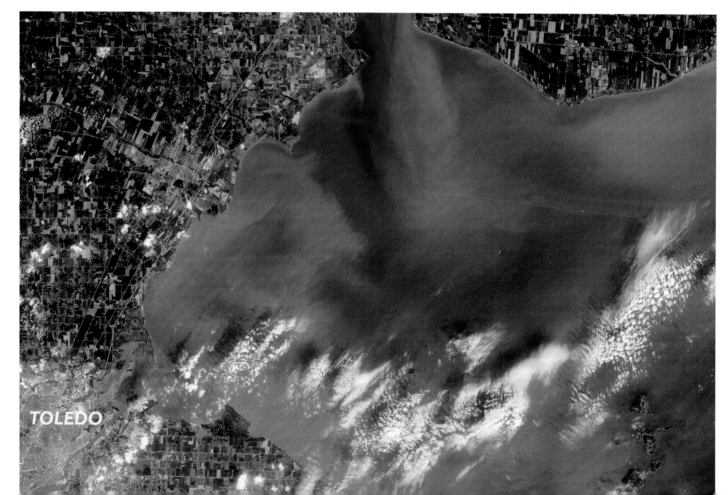

This image of western Lake Erie was captured on August 1, 2014 by the Operational Land Imager (OLI) on the Landsat 8 satellite. The greenish water is the algal bloom. (Landsat imagery courtesy of NASA Goddard Space Flight Center and U.S. Geological Survey)

TOLEDO

provides the food for tiny shrimp-like animals called zooplankton which in turn feed baby fish. But too much nitrogen and phosphorus will cause a lot of algae to grow, giving the water a visible green color or "bloom." Moreover, too much nitrogen and phosphorus also promotes the growth of the wrong kind of algae, blue-green algae like *Microcystis*, that may produce potent toxins. Phosphorus was believed to be the most important cause of algal growth and Ohio scientists noticed that since the mid-1990s more and more phosphorus had been entering Lake Erie. In 2007 they began to look closely at where that extra phosphorus was coming from. Looking at sources ranging from municipal sewage treatment plants, household lawn fertilizers, commercial fertilizer, and animal manure, scientists concluded that although there are many source of phosphorus, most of the phosphorus that was causing HABs in Lake Erie was coming from farm fields—from fertilizers being washed off of fields or traveling through drain tiles into waterways leading to the lake. And the watershed that was supplying the greatest share of phosphorus was the Maumee.

Although a harmful algal bloom sounds frightening, it doesn't need to be. The large size of the 2014 bloom briefly took the city of Toledo by surprise, but Toledo and other cities have been successfully removing HABs and toxins from our drinking water for many years and are continually improving their ability to detect HABs and to purify the water. Lake Erie HABs only grow in the summer months, therefore most of the year there is no risk of toxins in the lake. If you are at the beach and you are wor-

ried about HABs, a quick look around will usually tell whether you should go into the water. Beaches are tested often by Ohio state agencies and are posted if high levels of algal toxins are found. If there is no posted sign, look for the presence of a bright green scum along the shoreline with a consistency of a soft pudding or gravy. In the water, blue-green algae will also appear bright green and will often float on or just under the water surface. If you see these conditions don't go in the water and especially don't let any pets drink the water. Avoid hair-like algae that appears dark green / almost black, but don't worry about grassy sea-weeds or green stringy hair-like algae. There are plenty of photos of Lake Erie algal blooms online that will give you examples of what to look for.

Unfortunately, HABs are likely to be with us for many years to come. By using computer simulations and historical records scientists concluded that the amount of phosphorus entering Lake Erie needs to be reduced by about 40 percent on average in order to restore the Lake, beaches, and drinking water supplies to good health. It will take a lot of effort by all of us to reach that goal. The good news is that Lake Erie responds very quickly, within a year or two. As soon as we start reducing the amount of phosphorus entering the lake, the lake will begin improving.

Disposal of Dredged Materials

Another serious water quality issue is the disposal of materials dredged from the bottom of Maumee Bay. Toledo is a major port, hosting ocean-going freighters carrying grain and other cargoes around the world. To accommodate these vessels, a shipping channel at least 28 feet deep must be maintained. Yet, as mentioned in earlier chapters, Maumee Bay is extremely shallow—as little as only six feet deep during times of prolonged southwest winds. To maintain the port, the Army Corps of Engineers dredges tons of sediment from the channel. Where to dispose of these dredgings is a major controversy.

To date, there have been two methods of disposal, open-lake dumping and pumping into diked enclosures. Neither is a suitable solution. The dredgings are polluted with excess nutrients (especially Phosphorus, implicated in the HABs described by Dr. Bridgeman), pesticides, and other waste chemicals; open-lake disposal resuspends these pollutants and merely moves them from one area to another. Filling in the Bay by diking off portions and pumping in sediment is clearly unsustainable; Maumee Bay is a valuable recreational resource and important waterfowl habitat. In addition, enclosed dredged material can become anaerobic (lacking in oxygen) and then provide ideal conditions for botulism, a bacterial infection deadly to waterfowl and shorebirds.

Clearly, the ideal solution would be to return the dredgings upstream to farmland, which is where most of these materials originated. So far the huge volume of material and questions about its quality have made this option prohibitively expensive. But currently a pilot program is underway to see if returning some portion of the dredgings upstream might be feasible. The Toledo-Lucas County Port Authority received a $2.5 million grant to construct the Lake Erie Dredged Material Center for Innovation, now located along the Maumee River in north Toledo. Four 2.5-acre enclosures have been constructed to evaluate various ways of treating the dredgings to make them suitable for returning to farms upstream. We await the results.

Left: The 459-foot long lake freighter Evans Spirit.
(Photo courtesy The Toledo-Lucas County Port Authority)

Facing page: Dreging of the Maumee River.
(Photo courtesy *The Blade,* Shelby Cardell, 2015)

Invasive Species – Introduction

By Matthew R. Snyder and Carol A. Stepien

Ecological theory predicts that most invasive species should suffer from a founder effect—a loss of genetic diversity due to the introduction of a small number of individuals into a new range—which should decrease their ability to adapt to their new habitat. However, some species seem more successful in their introduced range than in their native homes. Recent work has shown that some of the most successful invaders experience no founder effect, owing to either a large number of founder individuals, or multiple introductions from several native populations. Alternative theories exist to explain the success of invasive species. When leaving their original habitat behind, they frequently escape their native competitors, predators, parasites, or diseases. It is also possible that invasive species more often are those that thrive in disturbed environments which humans provide in abundance. An additional hypothesis is that invasives may facilitate other introduced species, causing an "invasional meltdown" to occur in highly disturbed habitats.

Terrestrial Invasive Species

By Amy Stone and Kim High

When someone says "invasive species" what is the first thing you think of? Some may immediately picture an overly aggressive plant like Amur honeysuckle on its way to becoming a stand of a single species (monoculture), where it leafs out early in the spring, and remains green and in leaf late into fall, shading out all other plants. Others may think of the standing dead ash trees killed by the Emerald Ash Borer, a non-native insect that was identified in North America for the first time in June 2002 near Detroit, Michigan, and then discovered for the first time in Ohio in Lucas County seven months later. Some who have ties to water may suggest that Zebra Mussels be the invasive species poster-child, as it outcompetes other species and clogs pipes causing problems in our lakes and rivers.

While each person's experiences with invasive species may be unique, we can best battle these issues by joining forces to increase education and outreach about invasive species through general awareness, early detection, ongoing monitoring efforts and management options.

Invasive species are nothing new, but today's global society makes it particularly challenging to combat non-native pests. Today, there is a constant movement of goods around the world by air, sea and land. Many non-native species have "hitch-hiked," while others have been intentionally introduced for uses such as gardening and landscaping, agriculture, culinary pursuits and medicine. While it may seem that the United States is on the receiving end of these unwelcome guests, it is a two-way street, with the US both giving and receiving non-native pests. For example, our Fall Webworm, a native to Lucas County, is also known as the American White Moth in China where it is non-native and killing trees.

Whatever the source of introduction, management alternatives are typically difficult to devise and can be costly and time consuming. Approximately 50,000 non-native species have been introduced to the United States, at least half of which are plants. In Ohio alone, more than 700 plant species are non-native, and nearly 100 are considered invasive to the Buckeye state's natural areas. A relatively small number of our 50,000 non-native species are invasive; yet remarkably, those that are cause more than $120 billion a year in damage to agriculture, recreation, forestry, human health and the natural environment. You probably have personally experienced some of this monetary loss. When our region is hit by invasive species, the solution can come out of

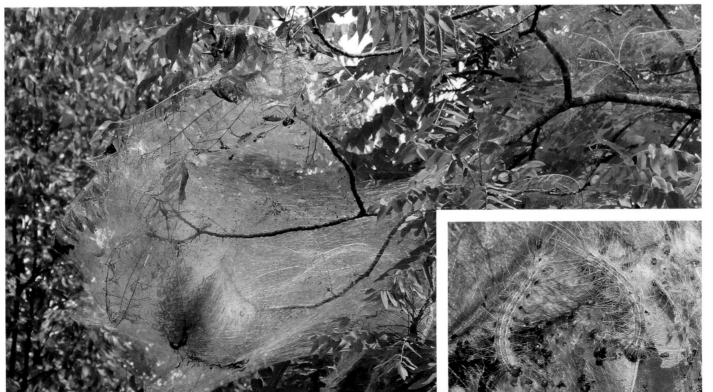

Above: An Emerald Ash Borer. (Photo courtesy Joe Boggs, The Ohio State University)

Left: A Fall webwork nest and a pair of fall webworms (inset) (Photos courtesy Joe Boggs, The Ohio State University)

your wallet directly, or through taxes that you have paid at the local, state or federal level.

What is an Invasive Species?

The National Invasive Species Council (NISC) was established in February 1999 to ensure that federal programs and activities to prevent and control invasive species are efficiently coordinated. NISC members are the Secretaries and Administrators of 13 federal departments and agencies. They provide high-level coordination on invasive species and are co-chaired by the Secretaries of Commerce, Agriculture, and the Interior. In 2001, the NISC defined "invasive species" as one that is (1) non-native or alien to the ecosystem under consideration, and (2) whose introduction causes or is likely to cause economic or environmental harm or harm to human health. This has become a widely used and acceptable definition.

Occasionally, people misuse the term invasive when describing an aggressive species that is native to an identified area (e.g., poison ivy, Boxelder Bug, or the fungus that causes oak wilt). The term "invasive" should only be used to describe a non-native or exotic species capable of causing harm as described above.

What is their Ecosystem Impact?

Invasive species exploit native ecosystems, usually to the detriment of native species. In the case of some insects, for example, indigenous species have co-evolved with their host and often have other bio-controls such as predators and parasites that help keep them in check. If these species are introduced into an area where this co-evolution did not occur, the host may have no resistance, bio-controls aren't present to help aid in the management of the species, and populations are able to grow rapidly, resulting in the emergence of a new invasive species. Invasive species can displace or eliminate native species, degrade and reduce natural areas and native wildlife habitat, and disrupt or destroy important ecosystem processes. Approximately 42 percent of threatened or endangered species are at risk due to non-native, invasive species.

Several emerging pests have been discovered recently in Ohio, including insects such as the Asian Longhorned Beetle, plants such as the giant hogweed, pathogens that cause thousand cankers disease, and white nose syndrome of bats. The sustainability of Ohio's forests, urban areas, natural areas and inland waterways is continuously threatened by what feels like a never-ending onslaught of emerging invasive pests.

Three Case Studies of Common Lucas County Invasive Species:

CASE 1: GYPSY MOTH

The Gypsy Moth was introduced to North America in 1869 by Etienne Leopold Trouvelot, a French scientist living in Medford, Massachusetts. Trouvelot wanted to breed Gypsy Moths with native silk moths in the hopes of creating a lucrative silk market in the U.S. He chose Gypsy Moths because, unlike silk moths which are very particular about what they eat, Gypsy Moths feed on leaves of over 500 types of trees and shrubs. He believed that a cross between these two moth species would create a hardy silk-producer that would be easy to raise and inexpensive to feed. Unfortunately for Trouvelot, the silk moths and Gypsy Moths are not in the same insect family and therefore unable to reproduce.

While Trouvelot was working with the Gypsy Moths, some of the insects escaped near his home in Massachusetts. He knew enough about Gypsy Moths to be concerned about their escape and reported the situation to the local authorities and even wrote about the escape in scientific journals but no one seemed concerned about a few tiny caterpillars, at least early on. Although this scientist's dream of creating a lucrative silk market here in the U.S. did not happen, he did unintentionally start another multi-million dollar industry that still exists today—the management and control of the Gypsy Moth in woodland and urban forests. Trouvelot eventually returned to France, leaving behind the Gypsy Moth which remains a pest in North America and has become an occasional reoccurring pest in Lucas County.

Insecticide treatments including aerial applications have been successful against Gypsy Moths and are coordinated through the U.S. Forest Service and the state departments of agriculture. Bio controls have also played a role in the ongoing management of Gypsy Moth populations, especially in between outbreak years. Gypsy Moths lay eggs on tree trunks in flat, fuzzy-looking rust-colored cases; these egg cases should be destroyed.

CASE 2: GARLIC MUSTARD

Garlic mustard is a member of the mustard family (Brassicaceae). It is known by several common names, many referring to its garlic-like scent and its historic use as a cooking herb. While garlic mustard is the most widely used common name in North America, this plant is also known as garlic root, garlicwort, hedge-garlic, jack-by-the-hedge, jack-in-the-

Gypsy moth egg case and pupae. (Photo by Eric Durbin)

bush, mustard root, poor-man's-mustard and sauce-alone.

Garlic mustard is native to Europe and can be found from England to Slovakia and from Sweden south to Italy. This plant has spread from its original range and is now found in North Africa, India, Sri Lanka, New Zealand, Canada, and the U.S.

Garlic mustard was likely brought to North America for use as a cooking herb, although it is also possible that seeds were accidentally introduced. The first record of garlic mustard in the United States is from Long Island, New York, in 1868. Since then, humans and animals have spread it across North America.

Garlic mustard is a biennial, taking two years to complete its lifecycle. Its young leaves produce a garlic smell when crushed. As leaves mature, the odor fades. In its first year, garlic mustard produces rosettes of dark-purple to green, kidney-shaped leaves with scalloped edges. In year two, the plants grow rapidly from the rosette to about waist high and produce triangular-shaped leaves with sharply toothed edges. Small white four-petaled flowers grow in clusters at the top of each stem and slender green fruits, called siliques, radiate outward along the stem below the flowers. Individual plants can have multiple flowering stalks and the number of flowers and siliques can vary greatly from each plant.

Garlic mustard can dominate forest understory communities. It will tolerate low light levels where other plants may be discouraged. Because it remains

A stand of garlic mustard.

green throughout the fall and into the winter and begins growing very early in the spring, garlic mustard has a head start on other flowering plants and tree seedlings. It outcompetes native spring woodland ephemeral plants such as liverworts, toothworts, Solomon-seal, trilliums, trout lily and many others.

Cutting, pulling, burning and applying herbicides have all been used to control garlic mustard with varying degrees of success. Control efforts must be done in early spring before the plant produces seed.

CASE 3: CALLERY PEAR (*example added by the author*)

Until 2015, the Bradford Callery pear was extremely popular as a street tree for new residential developments. It bloomed profusely in spring, and its foliage took on a lovely variegated crimson hue in the fall. Early cultivars of this tree were bred to be sterile—i.e., to produce a flower display but no fruit. However, it was soon clear that many pears were fruiting anyway, apparently due to genetic backcrossing with other varieties. Birds, especially European Starlings and American Robins, found the fruit delicious and spread its seeds across the landscape. The result was thickets of Callery pear invading meadows, parks, and other natural areas, crowding out native plant species. In addition, the tree was found to be weak-structured, easily splitting and breaking apart during wind storms or heavy snows.

In January 2018, the Ohio Department of Agriculture produced a list of 36 invasive tree species

Callery pear trees invade the prarie at Secor Metropark.
(Photo by Art Weber)

that can no longer be sold or distributed in Ohio. The Callery pear, so recently a favorite of many developers and landscapers, is on that list. No more can legally be sold after 2022, but unfortunately it likely will persist as a significant feature of our landscape far into the future.

An Insect to Watch for in Lucas County:
Asian Longhorned Beetle

A relatively new pest to North America, the Asian Longhorned Beetle (ALB) is an invasive species that kills deciduous trees. Even in areas where this menace has not been found, everyone is encouraged to check their trees for signs and symptoms of it throughout the year, and report any sightings of

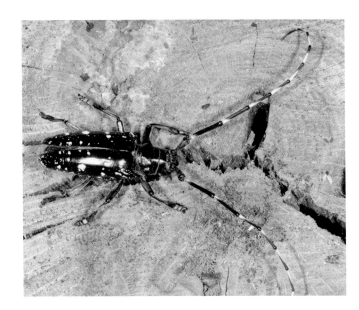

The adult Asian longhorned beetle is easily recognized by its long antenna, white spots, and white bands on its wings. (Photo courtesy Purdue Entomology, Jon Obermeyer)

a large black and white beetle to USDA. Eradication efforts have succeeded in states like Illinois and New Jersey. The goal is for Ohio to follow suit, and this is why in Lucas County, residents should be familiar with this pest.

ALB has a wide range of host tree species that includes twelve genera, with maples being the most notable. Once a tree is infested, there is no cure and the tree cannot be saved based on current eradication practices.

The ALB probably arrived in North America concealed in solid wood packing material that was shipped from China. Since its discovery, USDA did publish an interim rule in 1998, requiring all solid wood packing material from China be completely free of bark and also be treated with either preservatives, heat or fumigated prior to the arrival in the United States. In 2005, this rule is now in effect for all hardwood materials being imported from every country in the world as a means to hopefully decrease the spread of non-native species to other countries.

The small isolated occurrences of ALB in the U.S. are each unique infestations that came directly from China. In 2011, an infestation was discovered in southwest Ohio outside of Cincinnati in Clermont County. Continued efforts to eradicate this insect in Ohio are underway, as are efforts in Massachusetts, New York, and Ontario, Canada. Quarantines in these areas are established to prevent the spread of ALB.

The removal from the quarantined area of items that could spread the beetle, such as logs, trees, tree trimmings, chipped wood with pieces larger than 1 inch in two dimensions and firewood is prohibited by law.

A call for action – What you can do

You may be wondering, "What can I do to help wage the battle against invasive species?" Know that you can play an important role.

1. Stay updated on invasive species that are spreading into our area, or have the potential to make northwest Ohio their home.
2. Become familiar with landscape and garden plants identified as invasive, and avoid encouraging them. Even if they don't seem to be overly aggressive in your own yard, they could be detrimental to natural areas nearby, including woodlands and riparian areas.
3. Monitor for invasive species by using the Great Lakes Early Detection Network and consider becoming a Certified First Detector. Contact your local Extension Office for additional information. In Lucas County you can call 419-578-6783.

Remember, early detection and rapid response are paramount when battling invasive species. The longer these pests are ignored or not actively managed, the worse and more expensive the battle against them will become. Not all invasive species can be eradicated and eliminated, but efforts are more successful if new pests are identified quickly.

Aquatic Invasive Species in the Lake Erie Watershed
By Matthew R. Snyder and Carol A. Stepien

Great Lakes invaders come from a variety of sources. Most aquatic invasive species (AIS) became established in the region via accidental ballast water releases from commercial shipping vessels. Some invasive plants have been introduced intentionally as ornamentals for ponds and aquaria, and spread via fragmentation (breaking apart) or transport by boats and water birds. Other invasives were intentionally brought over and released for food.

A few species spread among the Great Lakes due to dispersal through the Welland Canal, part of the St. Lawrence Seaway, that opened in 1829 to bypass the natural barrier of Niagara Falls. This includes the first invasive species to be documented in the Great Lakes, the Sea Lamprey, which first appeared in Lake Erie in 1830. Since then, over 180 AIS have become established in the Great Lakes, leading to huge ecological and economic costs. In 2012, one estimate identified between $123 and $128 million in costs imposed by AIS upon industries and households annually in the Great Lakes region, and these costs are increasing every year. The following sections provide details about the most important AIS in the waters of Lucas County.

Plants

The common reed (Genus *Phragmites*) is a wetland plant native to the U.S. Atlantic coast as well

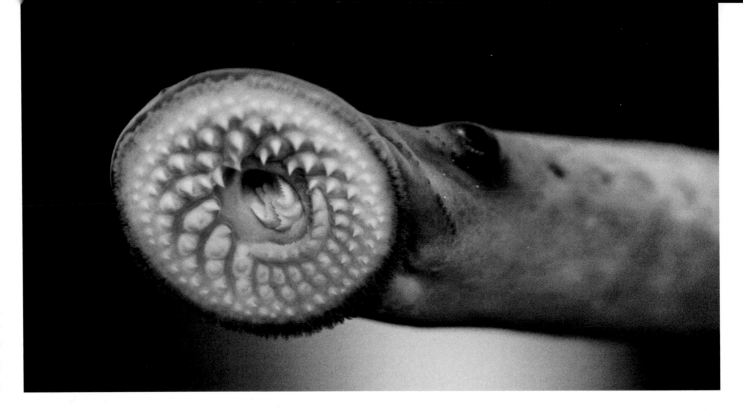

A Sea Lamprey.
(Photo courtesy Great Lakes Fishery Commission, Ted Lawrence)

as Eurasia. Multiple invasive genotypes were introduced in the late 1800s, likely by seed brought by European immigrants arriving in North America. Native *Phragmites* has always been rare in wetland plant communities and has a limited range. Invasive *Phragmites* grows more dense and taller, can occupy deeper waters, and now has spread throughout much of North America. In doing so, it has crowded out native *Phragmites* and other plants and provides less suitable habitat for wildlife. *Phragmites* spreads via seeds or clonally by growing new shoots from rhizomes, making control and eradication very difficult. Large amounts of money and man-hours are dedicated to removal of *Phragmites* every year.

Two species of non-native cattails are invasive, narrowleaf cattail and hybrid cattail. These species are common in wetlands and along rivers in the Great Lakes; their seeds were likely stowaways on ships that arrived early in the colonization of North America by Europeans. They form dense stands in wetland environments, crowding out native species. Cattails, like *Phragmites,* also grow clonally from rhizomes and from seeds. Cattails produce large amounts of seeds that are wind dispersed, making containing the spread of this invader very difficult.

Purple loosestrife, native to Europe and Asia, established in North America in the 1800s, likely as seeds included with dirt ballast that was used prior to the innovation of ballast water tanks. Purple loosestrife then spread throughout North America. It has been used intentionally as an ornamental plant, due to its attractive purple flowers. Purple loosestrife crowds out native plants and alters native habitat. It is a common weed in farm fields, and has spread widely in irrigation ditches. Several insects have been approved as controls for purple loosestrife, as they consume either the roots, leaves, flowers or seeds. Beetles in the genus *Galerucella* (also non-native) have been used very effectively to combat purple loosestrife in the Ottawa National Wildlife Refuge and other marshland areas in western Lake Erie.

Water milfoil was introduced through unintentional release from the pond and aquarium trade. It is native to Europe, Asia, and North Africa. Because it reproduces clonally, a small piece of milfoil can grow rapidly to cover an entire pond, and is very difficult to eradicate. As this invader comes to dominate surfaces of ponds and lakes, it blocks out light, killing native aquatic vegetation and drastically altering phytoplankton communities. These changes can cascade through food webs, affecting larger vertebrates such as fish and birds. Scientists are experimenting with biocontrols such as fish or insects that eat milfoil. It is critical that boaters and fishermen thoroughly clean all equipment where it was used to avoid transporting propagules of milfoil into new habitats.

Narrow reeds (top) and cattails (right). (Photos by Elliot Tramer)

Aquatic Invertebrates

The Spiny Water Flea is native to Eurasia and was accidentally introduced via ballast water from trans-oceanic ships. It first established in Lake Erie in 1985. This less than half-inch long zooplankton species competes with natives for phytoplankton food, and is undesirable fish food due to its long spiny tail that makes it difficult to eat. Genetic studies showed that this population underwent an initial founder effect, which then disappeared over time as new individuals joined the Great Lakes population from multiple sources. Another closely related crustacean zooplankton species, the Fishhook Water Flea, became established in Lake Erie in 2002.

A large crustacean, the Red Swamp Crayfish is believed to have been intentionally introduced into Lake Erie's Sandusky Bay in an attempt to establish a population for commercial harvest. This population, introduced from the Gulf Coast, was successfully reproducing by 1967. In Louisiana, profits from commercially cultured Red Swamp Crayfish exceed $150 million annually. Other subsequent establishments of this species in Lake Erie were either due to natural dispersal from the Sandusky Bay population or accidental release of individuals from aquariums. This species is common in the aquarium trade as its bright red color leads to advertisements as a "freshwater lobster." In addition, there is evidence that these crayfish can survive sewer systems and wastewater treatment, making it unlikely that it will be killed from flushing down toilets, which is a common disposal method of unwanted aquarium animals by consumers.

The Zebra and Quagga Mussels are two related bivalve mollusk species native to the Ponto-Caspian region (the Black, Azov, and Caspian Seas and their tributaries). The Zebra Mussel was discovered in Lake St. Clair in 1988, where it was introduced through transoceanic shipping through ballast water, and by 1990 had spread widely throughout the Great Lakes. The Quagga Mussel first was noted in Lake Erie in 1989, and can live in deeper water, frequently forming mats across the lake floor. The two species have established across much of the soft bottoms and hard surfaces of the Great Lakes. They may have facilitated the establishment of the Round Goby, which is another Ponto-Caspian invader, for which they are common prey. Economic impacts of the mussel invasion include fouling of intakes for water treatment and power plant cooling systems. Ecological impacts include displacement of native unionid clams and increased water clarity in Lake Erie. The mussels filter large quantities of water for phytoplankton food, thereby decreasing turbidity of the lake and altering the native food web. Genetic analyses of both species indicated no founder effect due to a large number of introduced individuals and multiple native source populations. The mussels have been spread all the way to reservoirs in California, due to overland transport by recreational boats.

The Asian Clam is another bivalve mollusk native to Asia and the eastern Mediterranean, which first successfully established in the Columbia River and then spread across North America and into the Great Lakes. It was introduced to the west coast of the US in 1938 either intentionally for harvest by immigrants or as a hitchhiker on the giant Pacific Oyster, also from Asia. The Asian Clam first appeared in Ohio in 1962, and has since displaced native unionid clams and resulted in costly fouling, especially to power plant intakes.

Fishes

There is some debate among scientists about whether the Sea Lamprey was native to Lake Ontario, where it may have established at the end of the last glaciation, or invaded after the opening of the St. Lawrence Seaway in the mid-1800s. The Sea Lamprey was not native to Lake Erie or the upper Great Lakes, as it could not have dispersed above Niagara Falls until the completion of the Welland Canal in 1829. It was found in Lake Erie one year after the completion of the locks. Since then populations of Sea Lamprey have exploded in the Great Lakes. This species is a blood parasite of large bodied fishes, and has significantly reduced the yield of several important fisheries such as Walleye, Lake Trout, and Atlantic Salmon. Currently over $14 million is spent annually on lamprey control, monitoring, and research. The most effective controls are species-specific poisons called lampricides that kill lampreys at early life history stages in river sediments where they spawn. Unfortunately, the lampricide applications also kill native benign lamprey species.

White Perch spread into Lake Erie from Lake Ontario by 1953. Fish eggs are an important part of white perch diets, including those of Walleye and White Bass. It competes for zooplankton food with the Yellow Perch and the young of many other fishes, and is believed to have negatively affected the western Lake Erie basin Yellow Perch population. It is known to hybridize with the native White Bass.

The Eurasian Round Goby and the Tubenose Goby invaded the Great Lakes ca. 1990, originally becoming established in the St. Clair River. Their invasion has also been attributed to ballast water transfer from ships originating from the Ponto-Caspian region, since genetic research has identified the source of the invasion as the northern Black Sea, in Ukraine. By 1995 the Round Goby had spread throughout the Great Lakes and is still expanding into tributaries. The Tubenose Goby has been slower to expand, appearing in Lake Erie in 2007 and remains rare. The Round Goby is a voracious egg predator and also consumes larval fish, zooplankton, and benthic invertebrates including Zebra and Quagga Mussels. Their feeding on eggs of Smallmouth Bass when the nest-guarding males were removed led the state of Ohio to shut down the bass fishery during the May to June breeding season. The Tubenose Goby has displaced the Rainbow Darter and Northern Madtom in many habitats, likely due to significant diet and habitat overlap.

There were no records of the Alewife, a small herring-like fish, in the Great Lakes until 1873, after the Erie Barge Canal allowed passage of fish from the Hudson River to Lake Ontario. The Alewife also may have been accidentally introduced to Lake Ontario with stocking of the American Shad. It was not observed in Lake Erie until 1931, invading through the Welland Canal. The arrival of Alewife in new habitats has been shown to restructure food webs, as they consume zooplankton otherwise available for native species. They have contributed to extirpations of Lake Herring and several chub species in the Great Lakes. Alewife did so well in the Great Lakes that their populations soon exceeded the carrying capacity of the environment, resulting in huge die offs that were a nuisance throughout the 1950s and 1960s. This prompted a reintroduction of another alien fish species, the Atlantic Salmon, which is a popular sport fish and a native predator of Alewife. Currently, Alewife is managed so that its populations do not fall below what is adequate to sustain the stocked Atlantic Salmon.

Rainbow Smelt is native to the U.S. Atlantic coast, as well as Alaska. It was intentionally introduced as a food resource to a small lake that drains into Lake Michigan in 1912 and soon after established throughout the Great Lakes, spreading to Lake Erie by 1935. The introduction of Rainbow Smelt contributed to declines in Lake Herring and Lake Whitefish. Rainbow Smelt also competes with native Yellow Perch and Lake Trout for food resources. The smelt's high concentration of thiaminase, which bioaccumulates in its salmonid predators, reduces these economically important game fishes' body condition and fecundity.

Rainbow Trout or Steelhead is a popular sport fish native west of the Rocky Mountains in North

A water snake dines on a Round Goby. (Photo by Art Weber)

America. Sportfish clubs and individuals have frequently introduced this fish throughout the eastern U.S., including the Great Lakes. One introduction took place in Lake Erie in the 1880s, and continues with stockings by the Michigan Department of Natural Resources, the Ohio Division of Wildlife, and the New York Department of Environmental Conservation into several tributaries. The fish return to the tributaries to spawn and spend the summers feeding in Lake Erie. In addition, there is some natural reproduction. The Rainbow Trout is a voracious predator that often outcompetes native fishes for food. It has been caught in the Ottawa River on the University of Toledo campus. The related non-native Brown Trout also has been stocked in Lake Erie beginning in the late 1800s. Brown Trout is native to Europe and competes with native Lake and Brook Trout for food and habitat.

Three other species have been stocked in the Great Lakes following the collapse of native Lake Trout populations due to overfishing, and the subsequent invasions of Alewife and Rainbow Smelt. These nonindigenous salmonids include Atlantic Salmon, Chinook Salmon, and Coho Salmon. Impacts of these introductions include further declines in native Lake and Brook Trout populations, and reductions in forage fish for native species such as Walleye and bass.

The exact year of introduction of the Common Carp in North America is debated but likely occurred in the early 1830s and was reported in Lake Erie by the 1880s. Carp are native to Eurasia. They uproot and consume aquatic plants and increase turbidity, thereby changing habitat in undesirable ways for several native species. They readily cross and back-cross with invasive Goldfish, and in some areas the resulting hybrids outnumber both parent species. Goldfish have the dubious distinction of being the first fish species known to be introduced in North America, in the early 1800s, introduced by settlers as an ornamental fish to ponds and lakes. Its Ohio introduction occurred as early as 1850 and since has become very common in the western basin of Lake Erie and its low-grade tributaries.

Grass Carp has been used worldwide as a biological control of aquatic vegetation. The species is native to Asia and was first introduced to the US in Alabama in 1963 and was first recorded in Sandusky Bay in Lake Erie in the 1980s. The Sandusky Bay population has long been thought of as a non-reproducing population that is the result of escaped fish from local ponds. Ohio law forbids the stocking of non-sterilized Grass Carp, yet recent research has determined that the population in Sandusky Bay is reproducing and spreading. This possibly is the result of less than 100 percent effective sterilization of the fish stocked into local ponds. Ecological impacts of Grass Carp are similar to Common Carp and Goldfish.

Disease

Viral hemorrhagic septicemia virus (VHS) is a fish disease that first appeared in the Great Lakes in 2003 in a single Muskellunge found in Lake St. Clair. The first outbreak in Lake Erie was in 2006, causing large fish kills. USDA APHIS prohibited inter-state transport of bait fishes as a response, unless they were tested and certified as VHS-free. Genetic analyses indicate that the Great Lakes strain of VHS is unique, originated in the Atlantic Ocean, and moved into the basin through the St. Lawrence Seaway.

VHS causes internal and external hemorrhaging in over 30 species of Great Lakes fishes. Other symptoms include erratic swimming and bloated abdomens, and infection usually leads to death. Viral particles survive for up to fourteen days in water and can also be transmitted when predatory fish prey on infected individuals. Yet fish to fish transmission through shed mucus and urine seems the most likely vector of infection as the virus spreads rapidly in congregations, especially during spring spawning season. In recent years, outbreaks have disappeared, yet some fish still test positive for the virus, which is rapidly mutating and may surge in the future.

Potential Future Invaders to Lake Erie

Eurasian Ruffe first appeared in 1986 in the Duluth area of Lake Superior. It has slowly spread to several areas, but so far remains in nearshore areas of the upper Great Lakes. It competes with the related native Yellow Perch for food and habitat. The Northern Snakehead is an obligate air breathing fish, whose juveniles can disperse overland. The species is native to China, Korea, and eastern Russia. It was discovered in Lake Michigan in 2004. Snakehead is a highly efficient predator on fishes along with amphibians, reptiles, birds, and crustaceans. It will compete with several native species if it establishes in the Great Lakes.

Silver Carp and Bighead Carp have been highly successful in their invasions in the Mississippi River system. Both species are filter feeders that were intentionally brought to the U.S. to control algae in sewage ponds and aquaculture facilities. Both species now have breeding populations near Chicago just south of an electric barrier. This electric barrier originally was constructed to prevent the Round Goby from entering the Mississippi River system, but by the time it was energized in 2002, it was too late.

Now it is the sole obstacle blocking the Silver and Bighead Carp from entering the Great Lakes. However, studies have shown that electrically-incapacitated fish can still be swept across the barrier in the wake of barges. Other work has shown that the presence of large metal barges can absorb enough of the voltage so that fish can swim alongside, freely passing the barrier.

Finally, the amount of electric current that enters a fish is dependent on the surface area of the individual, so small-bodied species can swim past the barrier. Three live Bighead Carps were captured in Lake Erie, but are believed to be a result of illegal releases and not an established population. If either or both of these carp species establishes in the Great Lakes, the consequences could be severe for native species. Silver and Bighead Carp are effective filter feeders that have been shown to drastically alter plankton communities, and in turn the entire food web.

Silver Carp in the Fox River in Illinois. (Photo courtesy U.S. Fish and Wildlife Service, Ryan Hagerty)

The Future of Invasive Species in the Great Lakes

The U.S. and Canada have adopted new ballast water regulations, requiring that any vessel entering the Great Lakes from the Atlantic Ocean flush its ballast tanks three times with seawater more than 200 nautical miles from shore, or retain its ballast water. Although under certain conditions some ships have been exempted from this requirement, since 2008 when these regulations were enacted, no new AIS have become established in the Great Lakes from overseas.

In 2011 the Army Corps of Engineers increased the voltage on the barrier in the Chicago Sanitary and Ship Canal with the intent that the increased electric current would stop all sizes fishes from crossing freely. However, in 72 recordings of ten minutes of underwater video taken after the voltage increase, schools of small fishes were observed freely crossing the barrier 61 percent of the time. While there is no evidence that Bighead or Silver Carp are currently crossing the barrier, it seems clear that the only effective way to prevent the spread of these species and others lined up on either side is to put in place a permanent physical barrier separating Lake Michigan from the Mississippi River watershed.

Stopping intentional introductions of AIS remains a very high priority, since many of the invasive species in the Great Lakes are the result of intentional introduction. Citizens frequently think they can improve habitat by introducing a species with a certain ecological role (e.g., Grass Carp). Others see introducing new species as an opportunity to provide society with food resources (e.g., Common Carp). Baitfish frequently escape or are intentionally left by anglers (e.g., Ruffe and Round Goby in "bait bucket transfers"). Still others see a potential for economic gain from the harvest of a non-native species (e.g., salmon species and Red Swamp Crayfish). Pet and aquarium releases are also very common (e.g., Goldfish and Red-eared Slider turtles).

The best weapon against all these well-intentioned but ill-advised introductions is education. The U.S. Geological Survey has a database of nonindigenous aquatic species (NAS) with fact sheets for each species including its invasion history, means of introduction, and impacts, all available for free online (nas.er.usgs.gov). The aquarium at the Toledo Zoo has a tank dedicated to the display of AIS in the Great Lakes, which is accompanied by information on the negative impacts of these invaders. The Ohio Department of Natural Resources runs an outreach program aimed at encouraging best practices among boaters and fishermen to stop the spread of AIS (ohiodnr.gov/stopaquatichitchhikers).

Early detection is critical for eradicating introduced populations before they become invasive. Predicting invasive species is difficult. Early detection of AIS with traditional survey methods often fails due to small numbers and elusiveness of invaders. DNA (genetic material) detection approaches offer a more accurate and efficient method of identifying rare species in a given habitat. All organisms shed DNA in the form of mucus, skin cells, and in their feces and urine. This DNA persists for a short time and is suspended in aquatic environments. Modern analytical techniques even allow researchers to detect the possible presence of very rare organisms in the habitat. It should be stated that DNA analyses are not without flaws. DNA can be moved between locations by predators such as birds or as mucus stuck on recreational boats or fishing equipment. In summary, cutting edge technologies such as DNA analysis combined with traditional survey methods provide powerful tools for early detection of invasive populations, when eradication or control efforts are most likely to succeed.

EPILOGUE

It is hard to imagine what northwestern Ohio was like when the first European explorers and trappers arrived. Few historical accounts provide insight to the grandeur of the hardwood upland and swamp forests. The immense Lake Erie coastal marshes and braided waterways of Swan Creek and the Maumee and Ottawa Rivers provided habitat for staggering numbers of fish and wildlife.

This tremendous array of natural resources provided both an impetus for and a barrier to the development and exploitation of the landscape. The Great Black Swamp was such a formidable impediment to land development that this region was the last corner of Ohio to be settled. But once the land began to change, it was rapid and to a large degree irreversible with the clearing of all forests, the draining of nearly all wetlands and channelization of countless small streams.

Somehow, something nearly miraculous has occurred. Remaining relic plant and animal populations have been discovered and protected. In many instances they have been nurtured and expanded thanks to decades of collaborative efforts to protect and restore examples of the landscape that were once here.

These examples exist, and will be sustained in perpetuity here in Lucas County, in the re-created areas of the Oak Openings Corridor, along natural riparian corridors, and along Lake Erie's shore.

Steven Madewell

NATURAL HISTORY RESOURCES

Lucas County is fortunate to have natural areas rich in plant and animal life, and a large number of organizations that educate, conduct research, advocate, and foster appreciation for our natural areas. Without exception, they are eager for the involvement of interested citizens, either as volunteers, interns, students, members, or simply as visitors.

Places to Visit

Metroparks of the Toledo Area – A county-wide park system consisting of sixteen parks covering more than 10,000 acres. The park system is gradually expanding as it purchases additional parcels. The Metroparks offers a wide variety of public programs for all ages, including guided walks, recreational activities, educational workshops, and abundant opportunities for volunteers to become involved in citizen research projects such as raptor and rare plant monitoring, vernal pool sampling, and much more.

5100 West Central Ave., Toledo, OH 43615
Phone 419-407-9700
www.metroparkstoledo.com

The Toledo Zoo and Aquarium – Recently voted as one of the 10 outstanding zoos in the United States, the Toledo Zoo has a variety of educational programs, state-of-the-art live animal exhibits, and is a leader in propagation of threatened species such as polar bears, African elephants, and several reptiles and amphibians. The African savanna and new aquarium are especially worthy of note.

2 Hippo Way, Toledo, OH 43614
Phone 419-385-5721
www.toledozoo.org

University of Toledo Lake Erie Research Center – Located on the shore of Maumee Bay, the Center is devoted to research on regional environmental issues, focusing especially on Lake Erie water quality and invasive species. LEC has a summer research program for undergraduates from other universities. It is open to the public during weekdays, and presents a series of evening public lectures by visiting scientists, as well as educational experiences for school groups, etc.

6200 Bayshore Rd., Oregon, OH 43616
Phone 419-530-8360
www.utoledo.edu/nsm/lec

Ottawa National Wildlife Refuge (ONWR) – Part of the U.S. Department of Interior Fish & Wildlife Service, ONWR was established in 1961 to provide habitat for waterfowl and other migratory birds, resident wildlife, and endangered and threatened species. It encompasses 6,500 acres along the shore of Lake Erie. Dike trails are open to visitors during daylight hours, and auto tours are offered on selected weekends. A variety of events and activities are offered.

14000 West S
R 2, Oak Harbor, OH 43449
Phone 419-898-0014
www.fws.gov/refuge/ottawa/
email ottawa@fws.gov

Magee Marsh Wildlife Area – Managed by the State of Ohio Department of Natural Resources (DNR), Division of Wildlife, the 2,200-acre Magee Marsh is best known as a magnet for migrating songbirds. Thousands of bird watchers visit the Magee Marsh Bird Trail each spring to see the warblers and other small birds on their northward passage. The adjacent marshes are managed for migratory waterfowl and are a popular destination for waterfowl hunters in the fall.

13229 West SR 2, Oak Harbor, OH 43449
Phone 419-898-0960
www.wildlife.ohiodnr.gov/mageemarsh

Irwin Prairie State Nature Preserve – Irwin Prairie is our best remaining example of wet prairie. Irwin contains 26 state-listed plant species. Managed by the Ohio DNR Division of Natural Areas and Preserves, the 200-acre prairie can be accessed by a boardwalk from a parking area on Bancroft Street west of Irwin Road.

www.naturepreserves.ohiodnr.gov/irwinprairie

Kitty Todd Nature Preserve – Located in the heart of the Oak Openings region, the 1,000-acre Kitty Todd is an excellent example of the globally-rare oak savanna ecosystem. Operated by The Nature Conservancy, it supports a number state-listed plants, habitat for the endangered Karner Blue Butterfly, and a diverse breeding songbird community. Much of the preserve is accessible by walking trails.

10420 Old State Line Rd., Swanton, OH 43558
Phone 419-867-1521
www.nature.org

Maumee Bay State Park – Operated by the Ohio DNR Division of State Parks, Maumee Bay (1336 acres) features a lodge and conference center (it hosts the Biggest Week in American Birding each May), cabins, and a nature center and swamp forest boardwalk. A beach on Lake Erie is open for swimming when water conditions permit.

1400 State Park Rd., Oregon, OH 43616
Phone 419-836-7758
Nature Center 419-836-9117
www.parks.ohiodnr.gov

Olander Park – A complex of five parks located near Sylvania, OH. The main parcel is 60 acres, featuring a 28-acre spring-fed lake. It Also features a paved 1.1 mile nature trail, and school programs.

6930 Sylvania Ave., Sylvania, OH 43560
Phone 419-882-8313
www.olanderpark.com

Toledo City Parks – 145 parks, athletic fields, and other open space facilities operated by the City of Toledo Division of Parks, Recreation and Forestry.

2201 Ottawa Pkwy., Toledo, OH 43606
Phone 419-936-2875
www.toledo.oh.gov/services/parks

Toledo Botanical Garden – A center for horticulture and the arts, operated by the Toledo Area Metroparks. Houses attractive flower displays and the Ohio State University Lucas County Extension offices. TBG sponsors an annual festival of the arts and Toledo GROWS, a community outreach horticultural program.

5403 Elmer Dr., Toledo, OH 43615
Phone 419-536-5566
www.toledogarden.org

Maumee State Forest – Located in southwestern Lucas County and parts of adjacent Henry and Fulton Counties, operated by the Ohio DNR Division of Forestry. Maumee State Forest consists of more than a dozen land parcels totaling 3,194 acres, and offers nearly 100 miles of trails, a windbreak arboretum, and a very diverse summer breeding bird community.

Phone 877-247-8733
www.forestry.ohiodnr.gov/maumee

Organizations

Toledo Naturalists' Association – Founded in 1933, TNA is one of the oldest continuously-operating nature clubs in the United States. Meetings are held on the third Saturday of most months and there are numerous field trips; non-members welcome to attend both. TNA publishes a monthly newsletter and annual yearbook and helps fund conservation-related research and land purchases. See the TNA web site for annotated lists of Toledo area plants and animals.

www.toledonaturalist.org

Black Swamp Bird Observatory – BSBO is devoted to education, research, and conservation of birds. Its banding station at Navarre Marsh has banded more than 100,000 birds in the last 25 years. BSBO organizes the Biggest Week in American Birding, now the largest birding festival in North America. Its headquarters includes a store with a diverse collection of books and other birding-related material.

13551 West SR 2, Oak Harbor, OH 43449
Phone 419-898-4070
www.bsbo.org

Black Swamp Conservancy – A non-profit land trust dedicated to protecting agricultural land and natural areas in northwest Ohio. To date they have protected more than 10,000 acres.

www.blackswamp.org

Partners for Clean Streams – A non-profit organization devoted to improving and protecting the area's waterways. PCS is the primary facilitator of the Maumee River Remedial Action Plan (RAP) and administers grants that fund water quality enhancement projects. A number of annual activities engage significant public participation, including "patch day," a storm drain stenciling day in spring, and a county-wide "clean your streams day" each September.

Phone 419-874-0727
www.partnersforcleanstreams.org

Wild Ones – A national non-profit organization with local chapters that teach the benefits of growing native wild plants in your yard. The local chapter serves all of NW Ohio and nearby SE Michigan. Monthly meetings September through May.

www.oakopenings.wildones.org

Lucas County Soil & Water Conservation District – A county agency that offers help to landowners in wise management their soil and water resources. Focuses especially on agricultural land use practices and offers a wide variety of educational programs and activities.

Phone 419-893-1966

Ohio State University Extension Service – Offers guidance relating to plant health to gardeners, horticulturalists and others. Educational programs and workshops. Horticulture information office located at the Toledo Botanical Garden.

5403 Elmer Dr., Toledo, OH 43615
Phone 419-578-6783

Toledo Metropolitan Area Council of Governments – TMACOG is a voluntary organization of governmental and non-governmental entities that have come together to work on quality of life issues that cross jurisdictional borders – specifically, those affecting transportation and environmental quality. TMACOG's Water Quality Council works to coordinate and recommend policies that will enhance and protect water quality in the region.

300 Martin Luther King Jr. Dr., Suite 300
Toledo, OH 43604
Phone 419-241-9155
www.tmacog.org

Oak Openings Region Conservancy – OORC is a non-profit land trust made up of citizens who want to preserve the Oak Openings region by owning and managing natural area parcels, helping landowners preserve Oak Openings species on their properties, assisting teachers with materials on the Oak Openings, and hosting educational programs for the public. OORC also oversees the Green Ribbon Initiative and serves as its umbrella agency.

Phone 419-867-0511

A Few Useful References

Anderson, M., E. Durbin, T. Kemp, S. Lauer, and E. Tramer, 2002. *Birds of the Toledo Area*. Ohio Biological Survey and Toledo Naturalists' Association.

Campbell, L. 1995. *The Marshes of Southwestern Lake Erie*. Ohio University press, Athens.

Field guides on a variety of plants and animals, by a variety of publishers. Good sources include the Peterson Field Guide series (Houghton-Mifflin Company), Kaufman Field Guides (also Houghton-Mifflin), National Audubon Society Field Guides, and National Geographic Field Guides (National Geographic Society)

Mayfield, H. 1976. *Changes in the Natural History of the Toledo Region Since the Coming of the White Man*. Metropolitan Park District of the Toledo Area.

Mushroom web sites (courtesy of Kim High):
www.mushroomexpert.com/taxonomy.html
www.ucmp.berkeley.edu/fungi/fungisy.html
http://tolweb.org/Fungi/2377
www.umich.edu/~mycology/links.html

Ohio Department of Natural Resources, Division of Wildlife. Field guidebooks. Excellent, concise booklets on a wide variety of common animals of Ohio, available free of charge from the agency.

Sanders, R. (ed.) 2001. *A Guide to Ohio Streams*. Streams Committee, Ohio Chapter, American Fisheries Society. Columbus, OH.

Thieme, J. (editor). 2016. *Living in the Oak Openings*. A guide to one of the world's last great places. The Nature Conservancy.

Tramer, E. 1988. *Effects of European settlement on the ecology of Lake Erie, 1795-1985*. In: V. Mayer and R. Fortner (Eds.), The Great Lake Erie. Ohio State Univ. and Ohio Sea Grant, Columbus, OH. Pp. 103-115.

INDEX